A Wolfe **OLD TIME STARS'** Book

Fred Rome's
POTTED PANTOS

Fred Rome's Potted Pantos are published singly by Reynolds Music. Catalogue and price list of these and other Reynolds Music publications can be had on request to Keith Prowse Music Publishing Co. Ltd., 28 / 42 Banner Street, London EC2.

Jacket illustration by Richard Hook

A Wolfe OLD TIME STARS' Book

Fred Rome's
POTTED PANTOS

CINDERELLA ☐ ALADDIN ☐ ROBINSON CRUSOE
DICK WHITTINGTON ☐ SINDBAD THE SAILOR ☐ BLUEBEARD
BABES IN THE WOOD ☐ LITTLE BO PEEP ☐ SLEEPING BEAUTY
QUEEN OF HEARTS ☐ LITTLE RED RIDING HOOD ☐ GOODY TWO SHOES

WOLFE PUBLISHING LIMITED
10 EARLHAM STREET LONDON WC2

ISBN 72340441 O

Reynolds Music Ltd. 1971

76-2812

Printed by Redwood Press Limited, Trowbridge & London

CONTENTS

INTRODUCTION

MAINSTREAM BRITISH humour has always had a healthy freedom from sophistication. The music hall, the variety stage, the concert party—even today's television comedy shows—have a tradition of broad, knockabout humour which stretches right back to the mediaeval folk plays and beyond those to the comedies of Plautus.

Whatever new fashion in comedy has come and gone, the main stream has flowed on. Much of the material, many of the situations, on British television in the 1970s are direct descendants of the romps in *The Canterbury Tales, Gammer Gurton's Needle* and *Ralph Roister Doister.*

Fred Rome—real name Frederick Herbert Toplis—was brought up in the mainstream tradition. He was both a performer and scriptwriter on the music halls, in concert parties and revues. Almost up to his death in 1957 at the age of 82, he kept up a prolific output of sketches, revue books and comedy numbers.

Fred's humour is neither sophisticated nor subtle. Nor would he ever have claimed it to be so. It was written for the belly laugh, not the polite titter or urbane smile; for mum, dad and the kids, not the West End first-nighters.

It is broad farce, slapstick . . . sometimes pure corn. But it lives. It belongs to the music hall world which is still very much with us. The world of the red nose and baggy pants, the world where virtue is always triumphant, where the villain gets his come-uppance, where the most desperate situation is resolved with a song and a chaste handclasp between hero and heroine, where disbelief is suspended to the point where a dance of fairies behind a gauze curtain is—if but for a few minutes—the only reality.

The twelve potted pantos were written as long sketches, for inclusion in concert party programmes, between 1925 and

1953. Every year thousands are still bought in their original single-volume form published by Reynolds and Co. Ltd.This is the first time that all twelve have been published together in one volume.

Part of the basic formula for any pantomime is the grafting of topical references on to an age-old story line. The social historian will find in the pantos a great deal which reflects the customs, interests and attitudes of the year in which they were written. The older reader, too, will find the thrill of recall in references to contemporary hairstyles, dances and brand names.

How much attitudes have changed can be judged by the treatment of Man Friday in *Robinson Crusoe* (1926). Here is the old-time 'coon' image...with Friday using the word 'massa' in almost every line, eating soap in mistake for cheese and tripping over his English at every turn. If Fred had written the panto today, Friday would still have been funny—but not at the expense of his colour.

No attempt has been made in this book to update the material. Not only would to do so be to destroy what value the pantos have as historical documents; it would also be to defeat its own object. What is topical this year will be out of date next year. The revisions necessary for a modern production of the pantos are best left to individual producers.

What is provided here is a collection of sketches which have stood well the test of time, which have been produced in countless theatres, village halls and pier-ends by both professionals and amateurs. Cinderella, for instance, has been performed for almost half a century...and it will be many years more before the curtain comes down on the final performance.

THE PANTOS

CINDERELLA

(1925)

CHARACTERS:
  Cinderella.
  Birdie. ⎫
  Baby. ⎭ Ugly Sisters.
  Buttons.
  Prince Charming.

SCENE: Hanging curtains, or an interior scene. A fireplace up back of stage, containing red paper to represent a lighted fire. Table and a few chairs. Clock at back.

OPENING MUSIC: Anything bright and lively—music to change to opening bar of ballad, such as 'My Garden of Flowers.' which Cinderella sings. If no drop curtain, Cinderella to enter on opening bars of song. She is dressed in a torn frock and appears sad. She sits on chair by fire for first verse—comes down stage for second verse. At end of song she resumes seat by fireplace.

CINDERELLA: *(Speaking with slight emotion)* I wonder why Fate is so unkind to me—why am I doomed to spend my life alone? I often picture faces in the fire like those noble lovers I used to read about in my Fairy Tales. I saw a stranger in the woods this morning who reminded me so of those I have read about. Ah me! But he too, just faded away and the fire within my heart went out. Perhaps some day I shall meet my Fate—who knows—he may yet look into my eyes and say 'Cinderella, I love you.' He may hold me by the hand and say—

(*Voice of* Birdie *is heard off-stage*). Have you bathed the rabbits yet?

CINDERELLA: (*rising from chair*) Here come my horrid step-sisters. I wonder why they hate me so?

(*Enter* Ugly Sisters, *both dressed in very eccentric style*)

BIRDIE: (*to* Cinderella) Don't sit there idling your time away when there is work to be done.

BABY: You know this is the day you have to polish the goldfish. Get some Goldfish Polish at once.

(*Exit* Cinderella, *half in fear*).

BIRDIE: You haven't wished me Many Happy Returns. You know I'm twenty-one today.

BABY: What again! You're always having twenty-first birthdays.

BIRDIE: I couldn't if I'd been born in Leap Year.

BABY: Leap Year! Your years are always leaping. You're always putting the clock back.

BIRDIE: I suppose you'll come of age when you're ninety.

BABY: What do you mean? I haven't got my wisdom teeth.

BIRDIE: I know, you've left them on the wash stand.

BABY: Don't be coarse. And don't throw my afflictions in my face.

BIRDIE: Face you call it. I've seen better looking door knockers.

BABY: Door knockers indeed. In my youth I was the Village Belle.

BIRDIE: You might have been a bell, but no one ever gave you a ring.

BABY: I had a proposal when I was eighteen.

BIRDIE:	It must have been a foggy day.
BABY:	You've never had a proposal.
BIRDIE:	Perhaps not, but I've had appendicitis.
BABY:	Yes, and you didn't know how to spell it.
BIRDIE:	Oh, stop it. I'm tired of this arguing. I won't have it. My mind is made up.
BABY:	And so is your face.
BIRDIE:	But, Baby dear, if you argue like this we shall both get so plain that we shall never get married.
BABY:	Don't say that. *(she begins to cry. Birdie cries—they both fall in each other's arms and sob).*
BIRDIE:	Don't let's make our faces wet, we'll shrink them.
BABY:	Let's have a dab of powder and dry clean them. *(they each produce a powder puff and powder their faces).*
BIRDIE:	You know, dear, we must see about getting a husband.
BABY:	Not *a* husband—we must get one each. If you get one and I don't, can he take me out on Thursdays?
BIRDIE:	Yes, if you keep him on the lead. Now how can we get a husband?
BABY:	Let's sing at the open window. A passer by may take a fancy to our voices and fall in love with us. Yes, we'll sing and let's hope someone is listening.
BIRDIE:	You talk as if you were a crystal set.

(Any humorous duet can be introduced here, such as 'I'm afraid we shall never agree,' or the following can be used).

13

DUET

(Air—'Comin' thro' the Rye.')

BABY: If a stranger hears us sing
          A pretty little lay,
          He may come along and ask us
          If we'll name the day.

BIRDIE: On no account seem over anxious,
          Look at him and sniff,
          And tell him, if he's wealthy,
          You will be his little 'wiff'.

BABY: Shall we both go on the stage
          And get in a revue,
          We might get a handsome husband
          In a week or two.

BIRDIE: I'll get offers from a Duke
          If I have any luck.

BABY: But if your husband is a Duke,
          Won't that make you a 'Duck'?

BIRDIE: If we sent our photograph
          To someone's famous soap,
          Got it published in the papers,
          That might give us hope.

BABY: We'll try Pear's and then Palmolive,
          Both would just be grand,

BIRDIE: And if they do not like our faces
          Let's try Monkey Brand.

BABY: P'raps we might do well in opera,
          I'm sure we should shine.
          As my voice is high it's in
          The 'upper attic' line.

BIRDIE: Mr. Beecham p'raps would like us,
          When he heard our trills.

BABY: He might then give us both a chance,
          Or else a box of pills.

14

BIRDIE:	Yes, I think opera is our mark—hear me wobble. *(does la la exercises).*
BABY:	I can do better than that. Hark! *(also does vocal exercises, but louder).*
	*(*Buttons *rushes on).*
BUTTONS:	What's the matter?
BABY:	We were just running over an opera.
BUTTONS:	I thought you were running over a cat.
BIRDIE:	You saucy worm—for two pins I'd—I'd stick them in you.
BABY:	Yes, my boy, with your cheek, you'll never get on.
BUTTONS:	And you'll never *get off.*
BIRDIE:	Now don't be rude, Buttons. You know how we both want to get married.
BUTTONS:	What sort of man do you want?
BABY:	I want one with a good record, a strong frame, a good talker—
BUTTONS:	You don't want a husband, you want a gramophone.
BIRDIE:	I want a tall man, curly hair, blue eyes, loving disposition.
BUTTONS:	I know a man just like that.
BIRDIE:	Buttons, will he marry me?
BUTTONS:	I don't know, I'll ask his wife. Do you want a sweetheart?
BIRDIE & BABY:	Yes!
BUTTONS:	I'll tell you how to get one. Go to the butchers, and buy a sheep's heart, and dip it in sugar. *Puts his finger to his nose and rushes off. He is followed by* Birdie *and* Baby).

(Slow music for Cinderella's *entrance).*
Cinderella *enters).*

CINDERELLA: Father has not yet returned. He is always out with some of his strange companions. How different when dear Mother was alive. I was no drudge then. Oh, why can't I have freedom like other girls? I suppose the thought of that handsome stranger I saw in the wood this morning, makes my poor heart sad. I will go there again tomorrow; he may be there too. But, there, I'll try and be more cheerful. I'll sing a song of love, and try and imagine my unknown lover is by my side.

*(*Cinderella *sings a love ballad. Many songs can be found to fit this situation. At end of song she sits by the fire.)*

(Re-enter Buttons*)*

BUTTONS: Ah, there she is. She is the apple of my eye, and I have got the pip.

CINDERELLA: Why Buttons, won't you come and sit with me by the fire?

BUTTONS: My heart is on fire already with love for you. My whole body is on fire. My heart is beating like a jazz band. My head is whirling like a roundabout.

CINDERELLA: Is that all love?

BUTTONS: Well, if it isn't love it's nettlerash. Will you marry me?

CINDERELLA: But I'm not sure if I love you.

BUTTONS: Never mind, I shan't be at home much. When we are married I'll take in washing for you to do.

(Birdie's voice heard off—Cinderella!)

BUTTONS: Oh lor, here comes one of the freaks.

(Birdie re-enters)

BUTTONS:	Well, now I'm going.
BIRDIE:	Where?
BUTTONS:	Home.
BIRDIE:	Whatever for.
BUTTONS:	Because I live there.

(Exit Buttons)

BIRDIE: Now Cinderella, don't sit there doing nothing. If you must do nothing, do it and get it over. I am going hunting in the morning and I want my riding habit repaired. I always have made bad habits.

(Re-enter Baby).

BABY: There is that Cinderella sitting down again. We spoil her, that's what it is. There never was a truer saying than 'spare the rod and boil the child.'

CINDERELLA: May I go in to the woods this evening to gather some flowers.

BIRDIE: Certainly not. What do you want to pick the flowers for—they haven't done you any harm.

BABY: If you want to do some picking, there's my pink dress, you can unpick that. I'm going to make it into iron holders.

BIRDIE: If you don't get on with your work I shall be picking a quarrel with you—so you can put that in your sieve and sift it.

(Exit Cinderella slowly)

BABY: That girl will send me right out of my mind.

BIRDIE: You won't have far to go dear, will you?

BABY: What do you mean? Now don't start arguing again, or I may forget that I'm a perfect lady,

17

and I'll drop this lily little white hand of mine right across that place where your face should be.

BIRDIE: *(Very annoyed)* How dare you! You—

(Re-enter Buttons and blows whistle).

BUTTONS: Half time. The Prince's valet is without.

BABY: Without what?

BUTTONS: I'll go and see.

BIRDIE: Show the gentleman in.

(Exit Buttons. Birdie and Baby start to arrange their hair. Buttons re-enters).

BUTTONS: This way please and wipe your feet.

(Prince enters, Buttons pushes him on).

BIRDIE: Buttons, what are you doing?

BUTTONS: What you told me to do.

BIRDIE: I said 'Show him in'.

BUTTONS: I thought you said 'Shove him in'.

(Prince bows to Birdie and Baby. They bow low)

BABY: Pardon our page, but he is only a menial.

BUTTONS: I'm only a what-ial? I'll have you up for in-flammation of character.

(Buttons, very annoyed, walks backwards and forwards at back of stage).

PRINCE: Excuse my calling at this late hour ladies, but I have an important letter from my master, the Prince.

(Birdie and Baby dance round stage in delight. Prince hands letter to Birdie, she is about to

read it when Baby *snatches it from her.* Baby *is about to read it, when* Buttons *snatches it from her and hands it back to the* Prince).

BUTTONS: Start again, your worship, that was a misdeal.

BIRDIE: *(taking letter from* Prince). Trust you'll pardon the rudeness of that urchin, but he has no manners.

BUTTONS: *(to* Prince) Pardon the meanness of that maiden, but she has no money.

BIRDIE: *(reading letter).* His Royal Highness commands the presence of the Baron's daughters at the royal ball to-night.

BABY: How jolly. That will be the second ball we have been to this week.

BUTTONS: Last week you went to Three Brass Balls in one day. *(a big bell is rung off the stage).* Pardon me, I'm wanted on the 'phone. *(Exit* Buttons).

BIRDIE: Will you tell Mr. Prince Esq., that we shall be delighted to accept his kind invitation.

BABY: Yes, it will indeed give us terrible pleasure.

PRINCE: But you have another sister, I fancy.

BIRDIE: Have we?

PRINCE: The invitation includes her.

(re-enter Cinderella)

CINDERELLA: I've overheard all. Do let me go. *(She looks at the* Prince, *then speaks aside).* It is my lover I saw in the woods.

PRINCE: *(Looks at* Cinderella, *then speaks aside).* The little girl I saw picking the wild flowers.

BIRDIE: *(to* Cinderella) Of course, you can't go.

CINDERELLA: Why not? *(calling off)* Buttons! *(*Buttons *appears at entrance)* Bring this gentleman some refreshment.

19

BUTTONS: What shall I bring? We only have raspberry vinegar, and a little brimstone and treacle in the wine cellar just now. *(Exit Buttons).*

BIRDIE: If you will excuse us we will get you your refreshments with our own hands. Come Baby.

(Exit Birdie and Baby).

PRINCE: *(goes up to Cinderella and takes her hand).* So at last. So the tale I've heard is true. They treat you like a drudge. But just wait, little girl. You shall be rewarded for the hardships you have had to endure, or my name is not Prince Perfect.

CINDERELLA: *(in surprise).* Are you a real Prince?

PRINCE: Yes, I am impersonating my valet to allay idle curiosity. But I have a sad heart too. So come let us sing our cares away.

(Here a love duet can be introduced between Cinderella and the Prince. At end of duet, Cinderella exits R. Buttons enters L).

PRINCE: One moment, my lad. Would you like a couple of bob?

BUTTONS: Would I what? Can a duck swim? *(Prince gives him coin)* Two bob! I didn't think there was so much money in the world.

PRINCE: Tell me, how do those sisters treat the pretty one?

BUTTONS: Treat her! They never treat her to anything.

PRINCE: No, I mean, are they unkind to her?

BUTTONS: Terrible. But I'm not going to stand it any longer. I'm going straight up to them and tell them what I think of them. *(He pulls himself up in a commanding way).* (Birdie's *voice off:* Buttons!) Oh lor. *(He saunters off, half afraid).*

PRINCE: So I have learnt the truth. But the little Cinderella shall be at my ball to-night at all costs. I feel already that Cupid is watching both of us.

(Re-enter Cinderella*)*.

CINDERELLA: Oh pardon me, Sir, but—

PRINCE: Don't be afraid, little girl. You need have no fear of me. Come! let us talk.

CINDERELLA: But you are a gentleman of courts, while I am but a humble girl.

PRINCE: No matter what our station, our hearts are the same. I want to be your friend.

CINDERELLA: How kind of you. If only I *could* come to the ball.

PRINCE: You *shall* come, little girl, or—

(Voices of Birdie *and* Baby *heard off. They re-enter)*.

BIRDIE: *(speaking as she enters):* I don't know if I had better wear my pruce pink, or that scarlet seal-skin dress to-night.

BABY: I think I should wear your purple green.

BIRDIE: My feet won't keep still with excitement.
I'm all of a dither.

BABY: Do let us dance *(to* Prince*)*. Do you know the St. Vitus?

(Buttons re-enters).

BIRDIE: *(Excitedly to* Buttons*):* We are going to the ball to-night.

BUTTONS: Are we all goin'?

BIRDIE: Yes. *(Clock strikes nine)*.

BUTTONS: Yes, and the clock's going too.

(They all take hands, and dance to any lively air or the following may be used).

Air—'John Peel'

BIRDIE: What times we'll have at the ball to-night,

BABY: We're sure to set the Town alight,

BUTTONS: If you don't wear masks, they'll have a fright
At the Prince's ball this evening

CINDERELLA: Oh, how I wish that I could go

BIRDIE: Don't be absurd, you're much too low,

BABY: They'll only have the elite you know,
At the Prince's ball this evening.

PRINCE: *(To* Cinderella*)*
Ah well, little girl, now don't be sad,
The time may come when you'll feel so glad,
When you hear the pleasure some have had,
At the Prince's ball this evening.

(Music repeated for dance).
(All Exit).

(NOTE—To convey that the ball is in progress, the hands of the clock start to move. This can be worked from behind the curtains at back of clock. Dance music can here be played, or a gramophone played off stage. If possible a few dancers might come on and dance with the lights lowered. This continues until the clock strikes 12. All lights up. Dancers disappear. Music 'After the ball').

(Enter Buttons*)*.

BUTTONS: Oh! what a night we had at the ball. And to think that the chap who came here and said he was the Prince's *varlet* was really the Prince— what a turncoat! It was very nice of the Prince to smuggle Cinderella in as he did. I hardly knew her in her ball dress. She looked like a little sparrow on a wedding cake. Well, she made me think of wedding cakes anyhow—Oh! how I love her. There's only one thing I like as

22

much and that is apple turnover. The thought of them makes me shiver with joy, and, talking of shivering, I had some lovely ices last night—you know, those big fourpenny ones—I had so many ices that I went to sleep and dreamt that I was being chased by strawberry ices off the coast of Vanilla. I did have a time at the ball—first I had a fox trot and then I had a sausage roll. *(Here* Buttons *can introduce some stories as to what people did or said at the ball, concluding with a humorous song. At end of song* Cinderella *is heard singing off stage).* Ah! she comes! I'll hide and maybe I'll be able to hear who she is thinking about. *(He hides behind curtain at back of stage).*

*(*Cinderella *enters).*

CINDERELLA: It all seems like a beautiful dream. To think that I danced with a real live Prince. When I look into his eyes they seem to say—'I love you'—but no, that could never be, for I am but a humble girl while he is a real live Prince. If only love came to us in real life like it does in dreams!
(Here Cinderella *sings a ballad—suggested song, 'Dance in a dream to-night,' or something similar. After song,* Buttons *comes from his hiding place. He walks down stage with his arms folded and speaks in a dramatic manner).*

BUTTONS: Ah! false girl—you love another—send back all those presents I promised you. *(About to go).* Farewell for ever—we shall meet again.

CINDERELLA: But Buttons, I have never loved you.

BUTTONS: What! You never loved me, and I let you stroke my silkworms!

CINDERELLA: *(Taking* Buttons *by the arm).* But I will promise to be a sister to you.

23

BUTTONS: I don't want you to be a cistern—er—sister. I had one once but she was cut short in her prime.

CINDERELLA: Did she die?

BUTTONS: No, she had her hair bobbed.

CINDERELLA: But don't take things so seriously, Buttons.

BUTTONS: I will,—I will go and throw myself in the river. O'River!—you will find me later with my ears full of tadpoles. *(Exit)*.

CINDERELLA: Come back, Buttons. *(Calling off stage):* Come back.

BUTTONS: *(Off stage).* Too late, I have committed suicide. I am dead all over.

CINDERELLA: Wait a moment, Buttons, I will come and give you a great big kiss. (Cinderella *runs off stage, R.)*

(Enter Ugly Sisters, *L.)*

BIRDIE: Oh, I do feel ill.

BABY: It was your own fault, you shouldn't have had ginger beer with your trifle.

BIRDIE: That trifle was no trifle. Did you dance after supper?

BABY: No, I couldn't, my programme was full.

BIRDIE: And so were you, Say Baby, Babies Milk food is what you want; real stuff to put you straight: Babies love it.

BABY: Good idea, I'll have some Cow and Gate. The Prince nearly asked me to dance last night. Fancy him being the Prince. If I had known that when he called yesterday I would have asked him for his finger *prints*.

24

BIRDIE:	I danced with one of the gentry—he was dressed like a king and all over gold braid.
BABY:	That was the footman, my dear.
BIRDIE:	Well, how did I know, you know I never did get on well with my geography.
BABY:	I am sure I spoke to a king. He was a nice man, and kept on speaking about his long reign.
BIRDIE:	His long rein—yes, he was the coachman.

DUET. *Air—'Excelsior.'*

BIRDIE:	That happy night, how quickly it passed, The time, it seemed to go so fast, That supper was a fine repast. Oh dear, Oh lor! Oh dear, Oh lor!
BABY:	How I enjoyed that splendid spread, That tipsy cake got in my head, I wish I'd had some gruel instead. Oh dear, Oh lor! Oh dear, Oh lor!
BIRDIE:	Ice pudding too, it made me grin, I fear that ice was much too thin, I sat on one and tumbled in! Oh dear, Oh lor! Oh dear, Oh lor!
BABY:	That sausage roll soon made its mark, I bit it through then all seemed dark. I'm sure I heard that sausage bark. Oh dear, Oh lor! Oh dear, Oh lor!

(Exit after duet).

(Prince enters, holding shoe in hand).

PRINCE:	Where can my little sweetheart be. I have not closed my eyes the whole night through thinking of her. This shoe is hers I swear, but if there is another dainty foot to fit it, I would be willing to make its owner my bride. I will not rest until I find its rightful owner. *(Kisses shoe).* What is amiss with me today? Can it be love?

(Here the Prince *might introduce a love song, but this is optional.* Buttons *re-enters.)*

BUTTONS: Ah, Prince, there you are then! I had made up my mind to go and drown myself, but it came on to rain so I came back for my umbrella.

PRINCE: I fancy I saw you at the ball last night.

BUTTONS: You did, your highness.

PRINCE: But how did you manage to get in—you had no invitation?

BUTTONS: I went in sideways, and they mistook me for a sandwich.

PRINCE: I have no doubt my presence here so early surprises you.

BUTTONS: No, not at all. You know it's the early worm that catches the bird—which of our three birds do you want?

PRINCE: That I do not know. I am looking for the owner of this shoe.

BUTTONS: *(Looking at shoe).* What a dear little 'trotter case.' Is there such a tiny foot in the world? I bet the one who wears that has a tight foot when it's on, but it can't be a 'pussy-foot' for they never get *tight*. I'll call in the two bits of female furniture. Ah, here they are!

(Ugly Sisters re-enter).

BIRDIE: Good morning, Princy—why have you called—have you run out of milk?

PRINCE: No, I have come to find the owner of this dainty shoe, for who ever it fits I will wed.

BIRDIE: It's mine!

BABY: It's mine!

(They both rush about excitedly, and both bring chair down stage, both try to sit on it at the

same time and fall on the floor. They struggle for shoe and both get very annoyed with each other. At last Birdie sits on chair, removes boot and struggles to get her foot into shoe).

BIRDIE: It's nearly on—it's nearly on.

BUTTONS: Try folding your foot up.

BIRDIE: I think I want a shoe horn.

BUTTONS: No, you want a pickaxe.

BABY: *(snatching shoe from Birdie and pushing her off chair)*: I'm sure it will fit me.

BUTTONS: We shall all have a fit if it does.

BABY: I've always been told I've got a pretty foot.

BUTTONS: That's not a foot, it's a *yard*.

PRINCE: I'm sorry, ladies, but I fear you are not the owners of that shoe.

BIRDIE: I think it must have shrunk.

BABY: I think if I put on my thin stockings I could get it on.

BUTTONS: Why it's too tight for your big toe, let alone your foot.

(Cinderella enters. Prince turns to her and offers her shoe).

PRINCE: Will you try the shoe?

SISTERS: It's too silly, it'll never fit her.

(Cinderella sits and puts shoe on).

PRINCE: It fits! It fits!

BIRDIE: Give me air, I'm fainting.

BABY: Absurd!

27

BIRDIE: *Nonstance!*

PRINCE: *(taking* Cinderella *by the hand and kissing it).* I've won my prize.

BUTTONS: I've drawn a blank.

CINDERELLA: *(turning to* Buttons): Cheer up, Buttons, I shall always be fond of you.

BUTTONS: What am I to be then—your husband-in-law?

CINDERELLA: Let us forget the past of sorrow and sadness,
Let our future be all joy and gladness,
I promise I'll be kind and true
To Sisters both and Buttons too,
So join our hands without delay,
God bless you all.

BUTTONS: Hip—hip—hooray!

(Music—'The Wedding March').
(Baby and Birdie *get big bouquets from off stage.* Cinderella *and* Prince *exit.* Buttons *puts on clergyman's hat and stands up back.* Cinderella *and* Prince *enter arm-in-arm.* Cinderella *is wearing bridal veil. They walk to centre of stage and then up to* Buttons. Sisters *throw confetti as* Cinderella *and* Prince *kneel. Curtain falls).*

ALADDIN

(1925)

CHARACTERS:
Aladdin.
Abanazar.
Princess.
Widow Twankey.

SCENE: Hanging curtains, or interior scene.
Large table up back of stage.

OPENING MUSIC: Anything bright and
lively, or 'Oh my, what can the matter be?'
Widow Twankey enters. She carries a large washing
basket and calls 'Aladdin' as she enters. She is
dressed in an eccentric woman's dress *(This part
should be played by a man)*.

TWANK: Where is that boy? *(Puts down basket by side of
table)* I am sure he will grow up to be a police-
man, for you can never find him when he's
wanted. There is all this washing to be ironed
and sent home before I can get my rent. *(Takes
shirt out of basket with a big tear in it)* There's
a 'rent' but it's not the kind I am wanting.
(Shows collar with frayed edge) Now look at
the whiskers on this collar, I don't know if it
should be bobbed or shingled. *(Shows sock with
a big hole in heel which she puts her hand
through)* Now I don't know if I am to call this a
sock or a mitten. It takes me all my time, to get
these holes clean. *(Takes out very large nightdress.)* Now this belongs to Mrs. Tiddlepush.
The first time I had this to wash I sent it back.
I told her I didn't wash tents. What a life! Now
that I am a poor old widow I am washing all
day long. When my dear husband was alive I
never washed at all. We had decided to start a

29

little business as dyers and cleaners, but he *died* and I've been *cleaning* ever since. But what's the good of being sad, as the poet said 'It's a poor heart that has no turning.'

(Here a comic song can be introduced, or the following might be sung to the air of 'Pop goes the Weasel.')

I'm a widow poor and old,
Not the least bit swankey,
Have to wash to earn my bread,
Poor Widow Twankey.

I have got an only son,
He's growing very lanky,
Though 'Alad-*in*' isn't *in*,
I'm Widow Twankey

At the tub I spend my day,
Washing sheets or hankey,
That is why I get the 'blues,'
Poor Widow Twankey

Sometimes when I sit and think,
Fancy I'll go crankey,
Then I'll be a 'luniac,'
Poor Widow Twankey.

(Calling off-stage). Aladdin! Where are you? Will you come at once? I want you to sit on the copper to keep the steam in—you know I've had to chop up the copper lid to light the fire; I wish the other 'sun' was out as much as you are, then I shouldn't have to use so much 'Sunlight' *(Calling).* Aladdin! Here am I straining my voice when I should be straining the greens.

ALAD: *(off-stage)* Mother!

TWANK: Ah, here he is—jump over the step, I've just hearthstoned it.

Aladdin enters. *(This part should be played by a girl, in boy's costume).*

ALAD:	Hullo, Mother—working hard again?
TWANK:	Yes, I have to work; I'm too busy to get the dole, and they won't send it unless I pay the postage. Where have you been?
ALAD:	I've been to the pictures.
TWANK:	Don't be silly, pictures are not invented yet—never mind, pretend they are. So you've been to the pictures; why don't you stop at home and look at me? Aladdin, you've been smoking; I can smell it.
ALAD:	No, Mother, I haven't.
TWANK:	*(Sniffing)*. Well, who has been smoking? It must be the chimney.
ALAD:	Is dinner ready?
TWANK:	What do you mean 'dinner'—there isn't a penny in the house until I get paid for this washing—unless you'd like a few fried soap suds.
ALAD:	I am so hungry—I could eat anything.
TWANK:	Well, why not *bolt* the door.
ALAD:	Is there nothing to eat in the house?
TWANK:	There is only one thing, Aladdin—it will break my heart to eat it, but we cannot starve. *(She cries. Aladdin puts arms round her to comfort her)*.
ALAD:	Cheer up, Mother—what have we got for dinner?
TWANK:	I'm going to cook the parrot.
	(Exit Twankey sobbing).
ALAD:	Poor old Mother. Poor old Polly. How I wish I could make Mother happy. I've tried all I know—I've hung a horseshoe over the door. I've always turned my money—when I've had

31

any—to the new moon—but no luck seems to come our way. I was thinking about my twenty-first birthday next week just before I closed my eyes last night, and then I had a wonderful dream. In my dream a fairy gave me a purse of gold. It was only a dream. How I wish dreams would come true!

Song (Aladdin).

Air—'*John Peel*'—*or another song could be substituted.*

Last night I dreamed the whole night through
That I had wealth and riches too,
I only wish that dream came true
Before I'm one and twenty.

My mind's made up, I mean to try
For fame and fortune ere I die,
All Mother's wants I'd pacify
Before I'm one and twenty.

I'd brighten up this dismal place,
Have lovely curtains made of lace,
And buy poor Ma a brand new face
Before I'm one and twenty.

We'd have a dinner tête-a-tête,
And servants to come in and wait,
And each eat off a real gold plate
Before I'm one and twenty.

And if I win my big reward,
I'll have a car, just like a lord,
And drive about in a real Rolls-Ford
Before I'm one and twenty.

And praps I'll wed a real princess
We'll make the neighbours look I guess,
With Mother in a new silk dress,
Before I'm one and twenty.

ALAD: Oh, wouldn't it be lovely? No more rissoles—no more kippers—no more—

TWANK: *(Off-stage).* Aladdin!

ALAD: All right, Mother; I'm coming. *(Exit* Aladdin*)*.

(Mysterious music, or 'Here comes the Bogey Man').

(Enter Abanazar. *He wears a big black moustache; he is of the villain type)*.

ABAN: I'm Abanazar—who'll 'Ab-aban-azar'—I'm a vill-a-in of the deepest dye—only deeper. Everybody hates me—I love to be hated, there is only one man hated more than I am—that's the income tax collector. Here I am back in my native village. I first remember this village when it was only a weed. When I left this place ten years ago they had it thoroughly disinfected. Why I have returned is because I hear there is a magic lamp hidden in a cave by the mountain side. I dare not go and get it myself in case the mountain should recognise me. Who can I get to do the dirty deed. *(Looking off)*. Ah! Aladdin—he'll do—he comes this way.

                  (Enter Aladdin*)*.

ALAD: *(Looking at* Abanazar*)*. Not to-day thank you. We have no rags, bones or bottles.

ABAN: What, don't you know me?

ALAD: Are you the man from the Prudential?

ABAN: I am your rich uncle.

ALAD: What, Uncle *Rich*-ard?

ABAN: No, I am richer than that.

ALAD: Well, lend me ninepence.

ABAN: I wouldn't insult you by so small a sum.

ALAD: Well, be thoroughly rude and make it tenpence.

ABAN: I know a cave where all is golden.

ALAD: Golden what—golden syrup?

ABAN: No, real gold.

ALAD:	*(Calling off-stage).* Mother—Mr. Rothschild is here.
	(Twankey *rushes on).*
TWANK:	What child?
ALAD:	Rothschild—he knows where there is a lot of gold.
TWANK:	All right, I'll buy it—where is there lots of gold?
ABAN:	*(To* Aladdin*).* Come, boy; I'll show you.
TWANK:	Can I come too? I want to pay the rent.
ABAN:	Well, you'd better wait for 'Lady Day.'
TWANK:	Lady Day—I don't know her. Who does her washing?
ABAN:	Come my boy, put on your hat, And soon you'll be an autocrat. When once you reach this treasure store You'll come back home with wealth galore. Inside that cave's a wondrous sight, You'll be a millionaire to-night.
TWANK:	You do recite nicely, do you know 'Christmas Day in the Workhouse?'
ALAD:	Oh, Mother, I do hope all he says is right—if so my dream has come true.
TWANK:	I think I'm dreaming now—I am sure I shall wake up in a minute and find the kettle boiling over.
ABAN:	Hurry, boy!
ALAD:	*(Kissing* Twankey*).* Goodbye, Mother dear—I shan't be long—I'll be back soon with all those chunks of gold.
TWANK:	If you get the gold buy me a packet of hairpins on your way back dear.

34

ALAD:	Well, Mother! bye! bye! *(Exit* Aladdin *and* Abanazar).*
TWANK:	Yes, buy me what you like *(She dances round the stage).* I'm going to be rich—I'm going to be rich. I think I'll go and manicure the hedgehog and make him look nice for the party. *(Exit* Twankey).*
	(Lights down. Mysterious music. Enter Aladdin *and* Abanazar).*
ABAN:	Yonder is the cave my lad—go, get the prize, 'Twill be a sight to greet your eyes, Here, take this ring, 'twill add a charm And protect the wearer from all harm.
ALAD:	Whatever makes you speak in rhyme?
ABAN:	They always do in pantomime, At least—in all professional shows, They write up poems for the 'pros,' That lamp is somewhere there about.
ALAD:	I think the lamp has just gone out. *(Aladdin picks up lamp from behind curtains).* Ah! here it is—I've got it—see?
ABAN:	That's right my boy—come hand it me.
ALAD:	But what's the haste?
ABAN:	You little scamp Do as I say, give me the lamp.
ALAD:	The lamp is mine, I found it here, Why do you want to interfere?
ABAN:	Well, if my wishes you defy You stop in there until you die.
ALAD:	I can't die here, for don't forget, I haven't done my homework yet.
ABAN:	Well, if you live 'twill be far worse, Your fate will be a life-long curse, Give me the lamp.

35

ALAD: No I decline,
               I found the lamp—the lamp is mine.

*(At the end of each of the following 'curse lines'
a loud chord should be struck on the piano.)*

ABAN: Listen lad! before I go,
               These curses on you I bestow,
               May goblins haunt you in your sleep
               And both your calves turn into sheep,
               May all your hair turn into hay,
               Your nose turn up the other way,
               May you find beetles in your bread
               And porcupines inside your bed,
               May you never have a moment's rest
               With horsehair in your undervest,
               May you get the cane each day at school
               And have a bath in boiling gruel,
               May you always have a cold and cough
               And sneeze until your ears drop off,
               And now my lad I'll say goodbye
               And leave you in that cave to die.

(Exit Abanazar)

ALAD: Oh, Nunky, you've a heart of stone
               To leave me in this cave alone,
               What can I do?—the very thing,
               I'll quickly rub this magic ring.

*(Rubs ring. Lights up. Aladdin looks around the place in sur-
prise).*

               I'm home again—that's mighty quick
               This magic ring has done the trick.

(Enter Twankey)

TWANK: So you are home again—where is all that gold
               you were swanking about?

ALAD: Oh, Mother! Uncle *is* a wicked man.

TWANK: I always said he was no lady.

ALAD: He took me to a big dark cave and left me there
         to die.

TWANK: You wait till I see him again—I'll spoil his
         pretty face. What was his idea when you were in
         the cave?

ALAD: He wanted me to 'cave in.' He stood by the en-
         trance the whole time and wouldn't come a step
         farther.

TWANK: He's not a 'step father,' he's your uncle.

ALAD: He's no uncle, he's just a nasty mess of a man.

TWANK: You wait till I see him again, I'll make him look
         like a jig-saw puzzle. You wait till uncle comes
         strolling home.

(Duet. Twankey *and* Aladdin. *Air—'When Johnnie comes
marching home.')*

TWANK: When uncle comes strolling home again. Ah!
         Ah!!

ALAD: When uncle comes strolling home again. Ah!
         Ah!!

TWANK: We'll put the bounder through the hoop
         And make his features loop the loop,
         He'll find he's fairly in the soup,

BOTH: When uncle comes strolling home.

ALAD: When uncle comes strolling home again. Ah!
         Ah!!

TWANK: When uncle comes strolling home again. Ah!
         Ah!!

ALAD: I'll let him see I'm strong and brave,
         I'll show him how he should behave,
         We'll place a wreath upon his grave.

BOTH: When uncle comes strolling home.

TWANK: When uncle comes strolling home again. Ah!
         Ah!!

ALAD: When uncle comes strolling home again. Ah! Ah!!

TWANK: We'll get our own back I declare,
We'll bow and offer him a chair,
He'll sit and find it isn't there,

BOTH: When uncle comes strolling home.

(A short dance can be introduced here)

TWANK: What did you find in the cave?

ALAD: *(Showing lamp)*. Only this.

TWANK: What is it—an old sardine tin?

ALAD: No, it's a lamp—but it's no good without oil.

TWANK: That's like your father, he was always brighter when he was 'oiled'!

ALAD: I think these lamps give good lights.

TWANK: We want some lights badly.

ALAD: Who for?

TWANK: The cat—she loves lights.

(Music heard in the distance)

ALAD: Hark! what was that?

TWANK: It sounded like a noise.

ALAD: It's music.

TWANK: It must be that cheese humming again.

ALAD: It's lovely music.

TWANK: Who's doing it—it must be Mrs. Floomtooshes' wireless.

ALAD: Has she a broadcast set?

TWANK: I don't know, but she's got a 'broad cast' in her eye.

(Voice off: 'Make way for the princess.')

ALAD: Mother—A princess!

TWANK: Dear! dear! dear!—tell her I'm out—tell her I've gone for a walk with the goldfish, or something.

ALAD: Fancy a royal princess with real blue blood.

TWANK: Well, give her a squeeze of my blue bag.

ALAD: We must ask her in, it's raining hard.

TWANK: Surely the princess doesn't mind a shower; her father has been 'reigning' for years.

ALAD: *(Speaking off-stage).* Welcome to our humble home.

TWANK: Be sure and tell her to wipe her feet on the mat.

ALAD: Hush, Mother! *(Bows as the* princess *enters)*

(Enter princess*)*

TWANK: How sweet she looks. My face was like that until it got kicked by a horse.

ALAD: *(Aside to* Twankey*).* Go away, Mother.

TWANK: *(To* princess*).* Excuse me a moment—I have an appointment with several kings and queens— I'm playing patience. *(Exit* Twankey*).*

ALAD: Ah, sweet princess, I am indeed proud to have the honour of addressing you.

PRINCESS: It is kind of you to allow me to shelter. Would you instruct my servants to inform me when the rain has ceased?

ALAD: Let me be your servant—let me be your slave—may I offer you a chair. *(Looking round bewildered at seeing no chairs).*

PRINCESS: Thank you, I would rather stand.

ALAD:	*(Aside).* Thank goodness. *(To* princess*).* I fancy we have met before.
PRINCESS:	But where?
ALAD:	Ah! now I know—your pretty face oft haunts me in my dreams—can I be dreaming now?
PRINCESS:	See here is my hand *(Offers hand).* I think you'll find it is real.
ALAD:	*(Taking her hand in his)* Indeed it is. Those dainty fingertips. *(He kisses them).* Oh, pardon me if I have been too bold.
PRINCESS:	No—no—I think it is just divine.
ALAD:	But I am but a humble boy.
PRINCESS:	But your heart is just as true.
ALAD:	If riches ever came my way, would you but share my life?
PRINCESS:	*(sighs).* I would indeed.
ALAD:	Can those words be true? *(Embraces her. They look off-stage).* I hope it rains for ever. Ah, sweet princess, this is indeed my lucky day.

(Here a love duet could be introduced for princess *and* Aladdin. *After the duet they both exit.)*

(Dramatic music. Enter Abanazar. *He is wearing a false beard as a disguise. He carries a tray of new lamps.)*

ABAN:	New lamps for old. New lamps for old. Lamps; I give you one of gold.

(Enter princess *with* Aladdin's *lamp)*

PRINCESS:	What is that I hear you say? You're giving nice new lamps away?
ABAN:	Yes, what you heard my dear is right, I exchange old lamps for new ones bright.

| PRINCESS: | I this old one will throw away, |
| | Aladdin picked it up to-day. |

| ABAN: | *(aside.)* The very lamp, I'll get it quick, |
| | *(To* princess.*)* |

Come give me that and take your pick,
These nice ones here are made of gold,
Far better than the one you hold,
Come give it me—don't hesitate,
Or very soon you'll be too late.

*(*princess *hands him lamp.)*

I've got the lamp now you can go,
The prize is mine.

(Aladdin rushes on.)

ALAD:	Here half a mo'
	That lamp is mine—and that is flat,
	I'll take the lamp and you take that.

(Strikes at Abanazar, *who falls.)*

(Burlesque struggle between Aladdin *and* Abanazar.*)*

| PRINCESS: | Aladdin dear, what have you done? |

| ALAD: | This lamp man is a *wick*-ed one. |

| ABAN: | Come close to me, Aladdin, before I die. I want to make a confession—send for The News of the World. I have been a wicked man—it was I who stole the canary's bird seed—it was I who cut off the cat's whiskers to make a crystal set—it was I who put the mouse in the marmalade. Forgive me! When I am dead I promise to be a good man for the rest of my life. Do you mind if I go and die in the pantry—it's cooler there? When you come and visit me in the cemetery don't bring a wreath of holly, but put a nice big tapioca pudding on my grave. Farewell for ever, we shall meet again—I die—I die—I diddle-e-i-die *(Exit slowly.)* |

ALAD:	Ah, princess mine, I saved you from a dreadful fate.
PRINCESS:	Thank you, my brave boy.
ALAD:	Don't thank me, princess—all I have done for you has been a labour of love.
PRINCESS:	How happy we shall be when we are wed.
ALAD:	Come to my arms, princess. *(They embrace.)*
	(Enter Twankey.)
TWANK:	What! at it again. I knew the weather was a bit close but I didn't know it was as embracing as this. Now uncuddle, you two; what will the neighbours say? Now, Aladdin, did you send your uncle to come and die in my pantry?
ALAD:	Yes, Mother.
TWANK:	Well, don't do it again. I hate people dying when I am busy—and who do you think is going to clear up when he is dead? *(To princess.)* Excuse me, my dearie, but are you walking out with my boy or just keeping company?
PRINCESS:	We are betrothed.
TWANK:	You are be—what?
ALAD:	Betrothed—the princess has consented to be my wife.
TWANK:	That'll be nice—then you can go on the dole—but what is to become of me?
PRINCESS:	You can come with us to the palace.
TWANK:	What, the picture palace? Can I have a tip-up seat?
ALAD:	No, Mother—The princess's palace.
TWANK:	Oh, my dear—I hope the beds are aired. Do you really mean it? My heart is all of a palp.

42

ALAD: This is indeed a happy day.

PRINCESS: Come, let us sing a merry lay.

(Trio for princess, Aladdin and Twankey. Any musical number can be introduced here, or the following.)

Trio.

Air—'The Wearing o' the Green.'

TWANK: *(To princess.)* Oh won't it just be lovely
When Aladdin marries you,
I'll be a real fine lady then and have no work to do.

PRINCESS: You shall have a maid to wait on you
And do all you require.

ALAD: You'll have no need to rise at six
To light the kitchen fire.

PRINCESS: You will have a dress of satin then
And everything so fine.

TWANK: Aladdin must have told you that 'White Satin's'
in my line.

PRINCESS: You'll drive out every morning
In a carriage and a pair.

TWANK: I'll sit there like a lady with my nose up in the air.

ALAD: Now, Mother, you must cultivate good manners
and good grace.

TWANK: If the servants do not bow to me I'll smack 'em
across the face.

PRINCESS: You must have a rather haughty air
Good breeding you must show.

TWANK: I've started breeding rabbits so
Of course I ought to know.

PRINCESS: I hope you know just what to do
When first you go to court.

TWANK:	I just look at the magistrate And say, ' 'ullo, old sport.'
ALAD:	But, Mother, when you meet the King Won't you feel out of place?
TWANK:	The first time that I meet the King I'll trump him with an ace.
PRINCESS:	Well, everything is settled now So let our joys begin.
ALL:	We are all happy now We're wearing o' the grin.
TWANK:	Well, that's that. Now, what shall I wear at the wedding. I think I'll have my Comona Twinked *(To* princess.) What will you wear, my dear?
PRINCESS:	Orange blossoms on my head.
TWANK:	And 'Cherry Blossom' on your boots. We shall look nice—I hope they won't mistake me for the bride.
ALAD:	Don't worry, Mother. *I* shan't mistake you.
TWANK:	There is no need to be rude, my lad. I might get married again yet.
ALAD:	Yes—when the bargain sale starts.
PRINCESS:	Of course you might get married, Mother dear.
TWANK:	There is only one thing that prevents me.
PRINCESS:	What is that?
TWANK:	Nobody wants me.

(Enter Abanazar)

ABAN:	How about me?
TWANK:	This is so 'suddin'—but I thought you were dead.

44

ABAN: No, I changed my mind. I didn't like the idea of dying on a Friday: it's so unlucky.

ALAD: Now look here 'Abby,' if I let you live you must promise no more of those cave tricks.

ABAN: All right, my boy; I'll be good. *(To* princess.*)* Do you think you could find a room for me in your castle—I'm very handy about the house, and I'm very good at fretwork.

TWANK: Yes—all 'fret' and no work.

PRINCESS: Well, let us live as mortals should,
And promise you'll be kind and good.
If you do that then all is well,
Within my castle you shall dwell,
Aladdin's mine—his mother yours.

TWANK: *(To* Abanazar.*)* Come on—entwine me in your paws.

ALAD: I've won a prize, a sweet princess.

ABAN: *(Aside.)* And I've drawn a blank I guess.

PRINCESS: Now all join hands and let us sing.
Let our voices have a 'wedding' ring.
We'll finish with a joyous ramp,
Thus ends Aladdin and his lamp.

(All join hands and sing a bright popular song for finish.)

ROBINSON CRUSOE

(1926)

CHARACTERS:
Robinson Crusoe
Mrs. Crusoe
Friday
Polly
Will Atkins

SCENE: Outside Crusoe's hut on the island.

MUSIC TO OPEN: 'Home Sweet Home.'

(Crusoe *enters*).

CRUSOE: Yes, another day and no sign of a passing ship. It seems years since I was cast up from the wreck on this lonely island, and yet by the notches I cut daily on that tree I have been here but a few weeks. The memory of that awful shipwreck haunts me still—and here I am doomed to spend the rest of my life alone, no, not alone, for I have my faithful old friend Friday. I christened him Friday as that was the day when I rescued him from the cannibals. Yes, the fates have been kind to me in many ways, for my wooden chest was washed ashore soon after I landed here, so I have got possession of my gun. Without that I should have starved, for even a cooked parrot is an appetising dish in regions such as this. It is no good getting despondent: the Sun tells me it is nigh on mid-day. I must consult my chef and select my today's meal (*Calling off stage*). Friday! Friday!

47

FRIDAY:	Yes, massa.
CRUSOE:	Well, and what have you been doing this morning?
FRIDAY:	Lots of work massa, lots of work.
CRUSOE:	And what have you done?
FRIDAY:	I have made your bed massa, and given you a nice new pillow of grass.
CRUSOE:	That's all right but you forgot to take the stinging nettles out last night, and it felt like sleeping on a pin-cushion—and what else have you done?
FRIDAY:	I have cooked the saucepans and blackleaded the soup.
CRUSOE:	(*Smiling*). You are getting a little mixed with your English, I fancy, Friday.
FRIDAY:	Yes massa you am right: I mean I cleaned the soup in the saucepan.
CRUSOE:	Poor old Friday, I am afraid you will never understand my language.
FRIDAY:	I know English quite all right. Listen. 'What Oh!' Dere!
CRUSOE:	'What Oh!' is hardly English—we *owe* no one— we are the only nation who pays. Now Friday, get busy, and don't forget it is bath night tonight.
FRIDAY:	Sorry massa, no bath.
CRUSOE:	No bath—why?
FRIDAY:	I swallowed de soap and am full of bubbles.
CRUSOE:	But how came you to eat the soap?
FRIDAY:	I thought it was dat bit of cheese you give me.
CRUSOE:	Ah well, go and prepare my meal, but don't try

and wash yourself with the cheese will you?

FRIDAY: No massa. *(Exit Friday)*.

CRUSOE: Another day nearly gone. When night time comes I can but hope to dream of my dear little sweetheart Polly—she is all the world to me.

Song Crusoe.

(Any love ballad can be introduced here, or the following words may be used to the air of 'She wore a wreath of Roses').

CRUSOE:

Far away in England my Polly waits for me.
Within my memory her fair form and face I ever see,
Always her voice is calling to me afar from home.
I never can forget her as far from her I roam.

Within my dreams she comes to me, into her eyes I gaze.
Recalling those dear memories of happy childhood days.
If only I could fancy that we could meet again.
What happiness 'twould bring to me and my heart would know
   no pain.

We'd share a hut together with only room for two
The clouds would pass for ever and skies be always blue.
The fates still seem to tell me she'll one day be my bride.
Then I will envy no one with my Polly by my side.

(Exit Crusoe).

(Friday *rushes on excitedly with photo in hand)*.

FRIDAY: Massa, massa, come here quick, as quick as you can't.

(Re-enter Crusoe).

CRUSOE: Why, what's the matter Friday—have you had a

fright? You are all over perspiration, you look like a leaky fountain pen.

FRIDAY: No massa, I picked up this picture face on de beach just now.

CRUSOE: (*looking at picture*). Good heavens!

FRIDAY: Good heavens, is dis an angel tumbled out of de skies?

CRUSOE: Yes, it is a picture of an angel—it is my Polly.

FRIDAY: What, Polly Parrot?

CRUSOE: No, *my* Polly. (*Presses picture to heart*). My sweetheart.

FRIDAY: *Sweet—tart—*do we eat her?

CRUSOE: No, but she is sweet enough to eat—bless her.

(*Kisses picture*).

FRIDAY: Do you know dat white gal massa?

CRUSOE: Do I know her? She will one day be my wife.

FRIDAY: Your wife for one day?

CRUSOE: No, for always (*Hands* Friday *picture, which he holds the wrong way up*).

FRIDAY: Am dis her face?

CRUSOE: Of course it's her face—you never saw one sweeter.

FRIDAY: But she has whiskers.

CRUSOE: What do you mean? (*Looks at picture*). Why, you are holding it upside down. (*Turns picture*).

FRIDAY: Ah, now I see, she am lubly, she am like a little singing bird.

CRUSOE: Don't you call my girl a bird.

FRIDAY: But she has wings.

50

CRUSOE: Nothing of the sort, they are her ears—but I can't understand how my Polly's picture can have got on this island. There must a stranger about. Go, get my gun. (*Exit* Friday). I must investigate this. (*Re-enter* Friday *with gun*).

FRIDAY: Your shotgun massa. (*Hands gun to* Crusoe). Don't like it much at all, he make too loud noise with his mouth when he go pop.

CRUSOE: Gun won't hurt Friday. Come on, follow me—there is danger lurking round—this mystery must be cleared up, if we die in the attempt.

FRIDAY: Friday don't want to die yet—he has not had his dinner.

CRUSOE: You shan't die old friend—I'll protect you (*Shouldering gun and standing erect*). Come, throw out your chest (Friday *takes bundle from inside his chest and throws it away*). 'Tention! Quick march!! (Crusoe *and* Friday *march off R. Commotion is heard off stage L. Lively music.* Mrs. Crusoe *enters*).

MRS. CRUSOE: Well, here's a nice how-d'yer-do—in fact it's more of a 'how-do-you-don't.' There are only two things I don't like: they are sausages and shipwrecks. If they had only given our ship some more Bovril it would have stopped that sinking feeling. I can't think why they call a ship 'she.' The one I have just left was no lady I can tell you, although I heard the sailors talking about the ship's stays. It's the last time I shall ever go on a ship. Before I go back I shall wait until the sea has frozen over and I shall *walk* home. You see it was like this, I mislaid my son Robinson Crusoe—so I went down to the QUAY, of course ignorant people call it 'key', and I said 'I think my son has gone to sea,' and they said '*What* has he gone to see?' so I said 'To sea—see?' But they didn't because they were halfseas over, so I jumped on board and made up my mind to take a tripe—er—trip to find Robinson and I told the *Crew-so*. So off we went singing 'Britannia Rule, the Waves' and 'Boiled Beef and Carrots.' Then the waves began to get very annoyed. They looked just like my copper does on washing day, great big waves with deckled edges and white frilling on them. Then all of a sudden I felt a bump—then all of another sudden the captain shouted 'We're on the rocks,' so I said 'Don't worry about me, I've been on the rocks for years.' Then somebody said 'A sail! A sail!, we are going down'—so naturally I thought as they were talking about a sale and going down, that we should soon be in the bargain basement—but it was nothing of the such which, we were all going down into the 'juice.' They lowered the lifeboats, the captain cried 'Children *first*,' so I said '*Third* class is good enough for me.' But before I had time to finish my crossword puzzle, there I was drifting towards this allotment or whatever it is called—this bit of land is in a disgraceful state, nothing but weeds, they are longer than my widows weeds and not made of such good material. I hate this place, as soon as I can find the park keeper I shall tell him what I think of it. Those who like sea trips can have them, give me a nice summer afternoon sitting beside the canal, watching the pretty colours on the water running away from the gasworks.

Song Mrs. Crusoe.

Any suitable song can be introduced here, or the following words may be used to the air of 'Little Brown Jug.'

I got aboard a great big boat,
It sprang a leak and wouldn't float,
The waves they rose up mountains high,
They almost reached up to the sky.

Ha, ha, ha, he, he, he,
I've never seen a rougher sea.
Britannia rules the waves they state,
I only wish she'd rule them straight.

The boat got damaged in the deck,
While we all got it in the neck.
Said the captain as the boiler burst,
Save the women and children first.

Ha, ha, ha, he, he, he,
I felt so glad I was a 'she.'
Then on a raft I quickly laid,
I looked just like a young mermaid.

I drifted for an hour or more,
And then I caught sight of the shore,
I said 'Hurray! this is good biz.'
So I got saved and here I *is*.

Ha, ha, ha, he, he, he,
It was a bit of luck for me,
I nearly had to rest my bones,
Down in the deep with David Jones.

(Dance and Exit R.)

(Enter Polly *L.)*

POLLY: So I am out of that awful forest at last—I was scared to death—all the trees looked like huge animals and the strange noises they seemed to make frightened me so. I kept on hearing a strange sort of tapping noise, I couldn't think what it was. At last I discovered it was my heart beating—it perhaps was half due to fear, and half due to the love I have for Robin dear—I should think I have about as much chance of finding him here as I should have of finding a needle in a haystack. *(Looking off)*. Why, who is this I see—there can be only one face like that in the whole wide world—it *must* be—it is—*Mrs. Crusoe.*

(Mrs. Crusoe *enters with hand up to eyes as though in fear*).

MRS. CRUSOE: No, no Mr. Blackman, don't eat me—I am sure you wouldn't like me—I know I should be stringy when cooked.

POLLY: It is only me Mrs. Crusoe—I'm Polly.

MRS. CRUSOE: Well I never, so it is. What are *you* doing here in this Jingle—er—Jangly—er—Jungle—I always get mixed up with my tenses. How did you get here—did you come by wireless or what?

POLLY: I have just been thrown up on this island—the ship has gone down and she is now a perfect wreck.

MRS. CRUSOE: A perfect wreck—so am I.

POLLY: Why, we must have been on the same boat, I didn't see you.

MRS. CRUSOE: No dear, I came inside a banana crate, it's cheaper travelling that way.

POLLY: But tell me, why did you leave England?

MRS. CRUSOE: Well dear, I had finished washing out my smalls, and I thought while they were drying I would see if I could find my Robin.

POLLY: *Our* Robin you mean—what made you think of him?

MRS. CRUSOE: Well I called at the small general shop at the corner to get some Robin starch, and it made me think of my son. So I jumped on the mud boat and here I are.

POLLY: No 'am.

MRS. CRUSOE: No 'am thank you, I never touch it.

(Crusoe's *voice heard off*).

POLLY: What's that?

MRS. CRUSOE: It sounds like a hedgehog calling to its young.

POPPLY: No, listen, that's Robin's voice.

MRS. CRUSOE: That's not a robin, that's a starfinch.

POLLY: No, no, I mean Robin your son, Robin my sweetheart.

MRS. CRUSOE: It can't be—he wouldn't leave his voice about here. But it might be—he often lost his voice when he was young.

(Crusoe's voice again).

POLLY: It *is* Robin's voice.

MRS. CRUSOE: Well he must be broadcasting, or else he has swallowed a crystal set.

(Enter Crusoe).

CRUSOE: Polly! Mother! (*He rushes and embraces* Polly)

POLLY: Dearest!

MRS. CRUSOE: Let's have a bit of him—he's *my son*—he is only your guiding *star.*

(All three embrace).

MRS. CRUSOE: (*Blowing whistle*). Half time! Now breakaway there.

CRUSOE: But I can't understand it at all—how did you get here?

MRS. CRUSOE: We had a terrible trip—the boat ran off the line, then it burst its back tyre, and the conductor gave me the wrong change.

POLLY: Never mind *how* we got here Robin. We are here that is all that matters.

MRS. CRUSOE: I feel so happy I could sing with joy.

CRUSOE: Don't sing Mother dear, it will bring the cater-
           pillars out.

POLLY: We *must* sing.

MRS. CRUSOE: We're going to sing.

CRUSOE: Yes, let us all sing—we are all so happy.

(*Trio. Air 'I want to be happy'*)

That's made we three happy,
Now we can be happy,
We are a real happy crew,
Oh this is just splendid,
With all our woes ended,
'Way out here in Timbuctoo.
Let's shout hooray, and we will all dance too,
Pleased that we've come smiling through,
We're going to be happy,
All of we three happy,
We'll make you all happy too.

(*Dance and all exit*).

(*Dramatic music for entrance of* Will Atkins. *He enters with
bits of grass, a few caterpillars, snails, etc., sticking to his
clothes. As he enters he is picking them off*).

ATKINS: What a filthy place this is. I've been crawling on
           my stomach for hours, and my doctor told me it
           was bad to take exercise on an empty stomach.
           I've had a wrestling match with two giant snails,
           I've been nibbled by gnats, bitten by beetles and
           manicured by a mongoose, and now my ears
           are full of earwigs. I only just managed to es-
           cape from the wreck. I sat on a bar of Sunlight
           soap and got *washed* ashore—this is the worst
           seaside place I've ever seen. Why they haven't
           even got a pier here. I think Mrs. Crusoe and
           Polly came by same boat, but they
           didn't see me; I was looking out of the portholes
           trying to find the sherry holes. But where can
           the ladies be? Perhaps they've been eaten alive

56

by wild worms—this place ought to be cremated. (*Looks about*). Half a minute, this looks like the treasure island—it must be the treasure island, I've got the plan in my pocket wrapped round my bread and cheese. (*Opens plan and looks off*). Hullo! who's this—it must be Mr. Nugget.

(*Enter* Friday).

FRIDAY: Do you want Massa Crusoe?

ATKINS: What! Crusoe here—gracious good goodness—goodness good gracious—what is he doing here, cultivating Bile Beans?

FRIDAY: Do you know Massa Crusoe?

ATKINS: Do I know him, of course I do—when we were boys we used to both suck the same piece of toffee. But who are you?—you look a bit sunburnt—what have you got to do with Robinson Crusoe?

FRIDAY: Massa Crusoe, he come in big ship—ship break up and ship break down—massa found me with de savages, who was going to cook me at the stake.

ATKINS: You look a bit overcooked already.

FRIDAY: Massa Crusoe saved my life—kind man Massa Crusoe.

ATKINS: I know he's a kind man, but what *kind* of man?

FRIDAY: He is a good man.

ATKINS: What does he call you?

FRIDAY: Friday, 'cos he found me on dat day.

ATKINS: Fridays are usually unlucky to me, but you look a smart lad. When my luggage arrives and you're feeling thirsty, you can lick off the labels.

FRIDAY: What are you, massa white man?

57

ATKINS: Me, I'm Will Atkins, otherwise known as Sir Bertram Brimstone—the beetle burned burglar of Bow. Ah, I hear footprints, someone comes, stick to me and you will get your reward, I am the man who invented holes in muffins. Come with me and I'll introduce you to a couple of dandy lions I went to school with.

(*Exit* Atkins *and* Friday).

(*Enter* Polly)

POLLY: I am so happy, for I have found my dear Robin safe and sound. That kiss he gave me was worth twenty shipwrecks—it all seems like a dream, but I am sure it is not a dream, for that squeeze Robin gave me would have wakened me by now, even if I had been in a trance. What a funny thing love is, to be sure. Anyway, it's awfully nice.

(*Here* Polly *can introduce any love ballad. After song* Will Atkins *enters*).

ATKINS: Was that a nightingale I heard, or a gale in the night. (*Sees* Polly). What Polly! Were you on the wreck? So was I.

POLLY: Yes, you've been a wreck all your life.

ATKINS: Don't say that. I may have been a bit 'at sea' but I have always managed to keep my head above water.

POLLY: It's a pity you did that, for your face could do with a wash.

ATKINS: Don't be unkind, Polly; you know I've always loved you with a fourteen-horse power love. Say you'll be mine and you shall have anything you like, under eightpence.

POLLY: I have no love for you, Mr. Atkins, I love another.

58

ATKINS: Give me your hand with all your heart.

POLLY: (*Smacking his face*). There is my hand, with all my heart.

ATKINS: So you refuse me?

POLLY: Yes—I am on strike.

ATKINS: Remember *gurl*, you shall be mine, by fair means or by foul.

POLLY: Try your *fowl* way if you like, I'm not *chicken* hearted.

ATKINS: Ha! ha! you can't defy Will Atkins.

POLLY: Perhaps my *will* is stronger—we will see, instead of 'Will' your name may soon be '*won't.*'

ATKINS: Come to my arms. (*Stands with extended arms*).

POLLY: Let me pass.

ATKINS: No, not before you say you love me.

(*They struggle*. Polly *screams*. Crusoe *enters and knocks* Will Atkins *down*).

CRUSOE: Take that. (*He embraces* Polly).

ATKINS: I've taken it—is there anything else I can take?

CRUSOE: Yes, take your hook and go away.

ATKINS: If there were any policemen on this island I'd call them, and have you removed by force. *(Gets up)*. How dare you? You great hulking brute, coming up to me and hitting me like this. *(Atkins hits himself in the face)*. No, it was harder than that, you hit me like this. *(Hits himself again)*. Why did you do it?

CRUSOE: Because I have a perfect *right*. (*Indicating*

clenched fist of right hand). I believe in *fiscal* policy—and don't forget if any one interferes with my Polly I tick 'em off.

ATKINS: So that's your *Polly-ticks.*

CRUSOE: Get out. (*Up to* Atkins *in a threatening attitude*): Get out before I forget myself. (*Holds up fist*) See that?

ATKINS: Yes, I can see it, but I don't want any bananas thank you—all right I'm going—I'm going into the woods to sit on the toadstools and chew caterpillars. And, remember, if I die I shan't half tell you off in the morning. (*Exit* Atkins).

CRUSOE: Well darling we've got rid of him. Now let us talk of love: it is so refreshing and it's about the only thing the government hasn't taxed yet. Love in a wood is so romantic; there is no one listening but the little frogs, and frogs carry no *tales.*

POLLY: And you still love me Robin?

CRUSOE: Love you darling—I worship the weeds you walk upon. Some day we shall get married, and you shall have a lovely Robinson *trousseau.*

(*Any love duet can be introduced here, or the following words can be sung to the air of 'Sweet and Low'*)

CRUSOE: Sweetheart mine—love divine,
For you my heart is pining,
Your dear eyes mesmerise,
Just like two bright stars shining.

POLLY: There's nought in this world I love like you.
Nothing but death dear can part us two,
No one else matters to me dear,

CRUSOE: I want only you.

POLLY: I want only you.

BOTH: You.

60

(After duet, Crusoe *and* Polly *exit. Enter* Atkins. *He holds out one hand all but one finger extended, this he has bent down-he looks at hand before he speaks.)*

ATKINS: That's a funny thing, I've lost a bit of one of my fingers. I wonder if Crusoe bit it off in the fight we had just now. I didn't notice it until I tried to scratch my head. *(Puts hand in pocket, on taking hand out again he has unfolded his finger).* Well, I never, it was in my pocket all the time. I am very glad I found it, otherwise I should have had to become a *short-hand* writer. Now I must be careful and think out my plans. If I could only find the treasure on this island, I should become so rich that I could have goldfish for breakfast, and dine late with the blinds up— and then perhaps Polly would marry me. I would then give Polly the rich minerals and make *Poll-an-eiress.*

(Enter Mrs. Crusoe).

MRS. CRUSOE: *(Aside).* Ah! here's the park keeper. I'll ask him what time the band plays. *(Going up to* Atkins). Excuse me—I seem to know your face, but I can't think who it belongs to.

ATKINS: It belongs to me, it was a birthday present from Mother.

MRS. CRUSOE: I see, a kind of birthday *mug*—were you christened with a handle to your name?

ATKINS: No, I'm a self-starter.

MRS. CRUSOE: Yes, you gave me a start when I first saw you.

ATKINS: But tell me, what are you doing on this island?

MRS. CRUSOE: I've just come to look at the tapioca trees, but the whole place is running to waste.

ATKINS: Running to waste—that's more than I can say about your figure.

MRS. CRUSOE: That's quite enough of that. I may be a bit bumpy about the dining room, but it runs in my family. The doctor has ordered me fish to keep me thin.

ATKINS: Well, you should have a couple of whales every morning for breakfast.

MRS. CRUSOE: I have also been told that dancing makes the waist smaller.

ATKINS: That all depends how tight your partner squeezes it—what is your favourite dance?

MRS. CRUSOE: The hopscotch.

ATKINS: I like hop-scotch all right, but I usually have hops only, I can't afford the scotch. Are you engaged for the next dance?

MRS. CRUSOE: I was, but I can't find my partner; I think he has gone to bed.

ATKINS: He must be a *sleeping* partner. Listen, the wind is whistling through the trees. I don't recognize the tune, but let us dance.

(Mrs. Crusoe *and* Atkins *do an eccentric dance—something of the Polka order—they dance off stage*).

(*Enter* Crusoe *and* Friday).

CRUSOE: Now to search for the hidden treasure. If I find all this untold gold, I will make you a present, my faithful old friend—whatever you ask for, you shall have. Just think of the one thing in all the world that would make you happy, no matter what the cost. It shall be yours—what will you have?

FRIDAY: I'd like a saveloy.

CRUSOE: You shall have a golden saveloy, stuffed with

	diamonds—you shall have a new-laid auk's egg for your breakfast, you shall have a bath in champagne—you shall have—
FRIDAY:	Don't say any more massa, or I shall heave a fit.
CRUSOE:	Stop here, Friday, while I go to my hut and get the plan of where these wonderful treasures are supposed to be hidden.

(*Exit* Crusoe).

| FRIDAY: | Don't be long massa, I don't like being here all alone, by myself. De birds might come and peck at me and think I am de blackberry bush. |

(*Enters* Atkins).

ATKINS:	Hullo Friday. (*Pats him on the back*)
FRIDAY:	Go away Mister man, I am waiting for Massa Crusoe.
ATKINS:	Don't look so hot and cross Friday, or I shall call you Good Friday. You come with me and help me find that hidden treasure, I've got the plans here. (*Takes plans from out pocket*). Crusoe's plans are useless—I have been to his hut and changed them for some old soap wrappers—Now what do you say, will you help me?
FRIDAY:	Nebber—you wicked thief man—give me de plans you stole from Massa Crusoe—gib 'em me. (*Grabs at plans*).
ATKINS:	(*Smacks* Friday's *face with plans*). That's that!
FRIDAY:	I will take *that*. (*They both have short struggle. Friday takes plans.*)

(Crusoe, *followed by* Mrs. Crusoe, *enters. Crusoe parts* Atkins *and* Friday)

CRUSOE: I have heard all—thank you Friday. *(To* At-kins). So you are here again are you?

ATKINS: Yes, I took a return ticket.

CRUSOE: Well all tickets have to punched. *(Hits* Atkins*)*.

ATKINS: *(Embracing* Mrs. Crusoe) How dare you strike me with a baby in my arms.

CRUSOE: Get out, go into the wood and sit among the other worms.

MRS. CRUSOE: Robin, where are your manners—don't call Mr. Atkins a worm, what would his parents say?

ATKINS: Thank you Mrs. Crusoe for those kind words.

(Atkins *and* Mrs. Crusoe *retire up stage and appear to be mak-ing love)*.

(Polly *Enters*).

CRUSOE: Well Polly darling, I have news—good news. I have found the plans of the hidden treasure. If I succeed in finding all these riches, I shall make myself king of this island, and you shall be Queen—and Friday, shall be the ace of clubs.

POLLY: But there is no need to stay longer on this dreary island, for there is a gun boat in the bay.

MRS. CRUSOE: A gun boat, I hope it won't go off.

CRUSOE: It won't go off Mother—without us.

MRS. CRUSOE: It will be nice to be home again, for I left the kettle on the hob, and I'm sure it will be boiling over by now. But what about the treasure Robin?

CRUSOE: *(With arm round* Polly's *waist)*. This is the only treasure I want Mother.

ATKINS: What about me?

CRUSOE: You, you are a villain of the deepest dye.

ATKINS:	No, I'm not really dyed, I'm only 'twinked'— but I will promise to be good on one condition.
CRUSOE:	Name it.
ATKINS:	Can I marry your Mother?
CRUSOE:	Well, that will be a *step-father* to happiness.
MRS. CRUSOE:	(*Embracing* Atkins). Oh! this is so sudden, but we girls must have our fling, so fling your arms around me 'Attie' dear.

(Mrs. Crusoe *and* Atkins *embrace*).

ATKINS:	Do I remind you of Owen Nares?
MRS. CRUSOE:	No, Dirty Dick.
CRUSOE:	Now for the boat.
FRIDAY:	Oh massa! Are you going to leave poor old Friday to die here alone?
CRUSOE:	No, my brave old fellow, you come with us, we are not going to desert you now.
FRIDAY:	Oh massa, I'm so happy.
MRS. CRUSOE:	Yes, take Friday home with us Robin, it will make the neighbours think we've always got the sweep.
CRUSOE:	All right Mother, but break away there. (Mrs. Crusoe *stops embracing* Atkins).
MRS. CRUSOE:	All right Robin, but remember you were young yourself once.
POLLY:	There is no time to be lost.
CRUSOE:	Come Polly, come Friday, come Mother—
ATKINS:	(*To* Mrs. Crusoe. *Singing*). 'Come birdie, come and live with me.'
CRUSOE:	Now for England.
POLLY:	Home.

MRS. CRUSOE: *(Looking coy).* And Beauty.

(Air 'Death of Nelson').

CRUSOE:

For England, Home and Beauty,

MRS. CRUSOE:

feel so fresh and fruity.

CRUSOE:

Mother has got me a new Dad too,
So let us do our duty *(Crusoe kisses Polly. Atkins kisses
Mrs. Crusoe)*
And now for Home and Beauty.

(Into final chorus air—'Sailing.')

ALL:

Sailing, sailing, soon we'll be on the main,
We all shall be so bright and gay when we get home again.
Sailing, sailing for we are all merry and bright,
We hope you've all enjoyd yourself so wish you all
good night.

(Dance to air of 'Sailor's Hornpipe.')

Curtain.

DICK WHITTINGTON

(1927)

CHARACTERS:
Dick Whittington.
Alice.
Fitzwarren.
Eliza (the cook).
Jack (the idle apprentice).

SCENE: On Highgate Hill. Curtains. Milestone up back marked 'To London V. Miles.' Bright music for opening. Dick enters carrying bundle on stick flung over his shoulder.

DICK: Though christened 'Richard Whittington,' that name I couldn't stick,
For things were *hard,* I wasn't *rich,* so changed my name to 'Dick.'
I worked for old Fitzwarren, so my board and lodging made,
The only *board* he gave me was the bed on which I laid,
And often when I went to bed with hunger I was sore,
So to satisfy my appetite I had to *bolt* the door.
For breakfast I had scarce enough to satisfy a gnat,
As I was almost starving then, I had to eat my cat.
It broke my heart to do it, for I'd nothing else for sup.
And as poor puss laid on the dish, she too looked quite 'cut up,'
So that is why there is no cat that should be found with me,
That ends the *tail* of poor old puss—a sad *'Cat-as*-trophy.'

67

I've left Fitzwarren's shop for good, but my
heart's still aflame
Through thinking of his daughter—sweet Alice
is her name.
I'm walking on to London now, it's there that I
am told
Where riches in abundance lay and streets are
paved with gold.
I think I'll sit down awhile and rest my weary
bones,
(Distant bells)
How gay and bright those church bells sound.
how joyous are their tones,
But hark! those bells all seem to speak and call
me by my name,
It sounds to me like 'Turn again' those distant
bells exclaim.
I'm sure the words 'Dick Whittington' are ring-
ing in the air,
Yes 'Turn Again, Dick Whittington—Dick
Whittington, Lord Mayor.'
It's wonderful those distant bells can send their
welcome chime,
It cannot, of course, be wireless, for it's years
before its time!
But there, I must be dreaming—It's all a big
mistake,
I'd better try and sing a song to keep myself
awake.

SONG.

Any song can be introduced here or the following may be used:
Air—'Oh, my, what can the matter be?'

Oh, my, what can the matter be?
What can this musical clatter be,
Those bells are trying to flatter me,
Cheering me in my despair.
While on that milestone just now I was sitting
on,
Listening to bells as the hours they were flitting
on,
But how did those bells know my name was

Dick Whittington,
Saying I'd be a Lord Mayor?
Those bells they tell me to turn again,
Luck perhaps I shall earn again,
If so, how I shall yearn again,
    Alice to have by my side.
The doings of Whittington none shall disparage
If ever I ride in a swell Lord Mayor's carriage,
You all are invited to witness the marriage,
    When Alice Fitzwarren's my bride.

But what am I saying? It is all too beautiful to
be true. I suppose I am having daydreams. How
dare a poor lad like myself ever think that I
could call Alice—wife. *(Pulling himself up and
tapping himself on the chest)* 'Nil Desperan-
dum'—I don't quite know what that means, but
I used to write it in my exercise book at school.
I think it means if you can't get your sums right,
add them up again. But what did King Bruce
learn from the spider? Why, he said to the spider 'Go away—there are no flies on me.' Yes, I
will turn again, as the distant bells bade me. It is
a sign of good fortune to have bells ringing in
your ears. I wonder if good fortune really is
awaiting me? I will turn again and see. *(He
closes his eyes, turns and walks with extended
arms towards entrance R. As he does so* Alice
enters. She walks straight into Dick's *extended
arms.* Dick *closes his arms round her neck, then
opens his eyes.)* Alice!

ALICE: Dick! *(They embrace again)* Why are you going
away?

DICK: To seek my fortune in London Town.

ALICE: Ah! Dick dear, I fancy you have been reading
those fairy stories again. It is not so easy to become wealthy in London as you may imagine.

DICK: Well, then I shall go to sea—explore the mighty
ocean until I discover a treasure island where
riches *are* to be found.

ALICE:	I've heard that tale before— It's been the plan of many a man To leave their homes behind them, And go to share some riches rare, But very seldom find them.
DICK:	But Alice, you don't understand. As I sat on yonder stone just now, the distant bells they spoke to me—they seem to know.
ALICE:	No Dick, bells don't *talk*—they are only 'tolled.'
DICK:	I tell you Alice, those bells distinctly told me to 'Turn again,' and if I did I should one day become a big man.
ALICE:	*(Laughs)* Fancy you listening to the ringing of bells.
DICK:	There is one *belle* I should like to *ring*.
ALICE:	What bell is that?
DICK:	You are the *belle* I should like to *ring*—just a plain gold ring. *(Points to second finger on Alice's left hand. Love duet to be introduced here. The following words may be used. Air: 'Barcarolle' ('Tales of Hoffmann.')*
DICK:	Alice dear, my love's sincere, I love you with all my heart, You're just divine, just say you'll be mine And never again to part.
ALICE:	When you reach that foreign shore, And other maids have met, You may find two eyes so bright, That mine you may forget.
DICK:	I'll think dear all the time, Just of you sweetheart mine, Just wishing for the time To soon speed on its way.
BOTH:	Sweetheart mine. Sweetheart mine, Ah— Think of me. I'll think of you

Wherever we chance to be,
I swear my love by the stars up above
That you are my star of love,
Shining star from above
You are my star of love.
Yes—my Heaven—my all—my all—my love.

(Exit Alice and Dick, R. Enter Eliza, the Cook, L. She is carrying a roast chicken wrapped up in paper.)

ELIZA: Before I tell you who I am you'd better have a look.

No, my name's not Phyllis Dare. I'm old Fitz-warren's Cook,

I've come out for a picnic and I've cooked myself a 'chick'.

I'm going to sit and *pick* the chick, the rest I'm going to 'nick.'

Young Idle Jack came out with me, but don't know where he is,

He's put his two feet in a pond and bathing them in 'Tiz,'

There's lots I want to tell you, but hate this silly rhyme,

So let me talk like real cooks do—it saves a lot of time.

You see I'm Fitzwarren's cook—and *what* a cook. I cook his breakfast in the mornings, and I cook his books in the afternoons, and I cook the cuckoo clock for supper, and that's how I *save time.* Fitzwarren is a funny name, his mother's real name was Warren, but her son had fits so they called him *Fitz-Warren.* Her sister was a wardrobe dealer, so they called her *Miss Fits.* My master can wear anyone's clothes, so anything fits Warren. I've been working for the Fitzwarren family for about 50 years on and off—mostly *off.* They wanted a *plain* cook so they engaged me. I understand cooking, my father was a chef, my mother was

71

a *Chiffonier*. You should taste some of my special dishes—they're lovely. Now my filletted saus-*ar*-ges, they are the talk of the place. Quite simple to make—you just take a sausage and grab it by the throat and stab it in the dado with a tin-opener, cut away its overcoat and empty it—you always have to *empty* to *fill-et*, that sounds wrong, empty to fill it, am I speaking left-handed? Anyhow you've now got the sausage skinned to death, then you put the skin in a saucepan—a clean saucepan if possible, and bring the skin to a boil, the bigger the boil the more tender the skin: you know that if you've ever had a boil on the neck. Then you serve with Zam-Buk sauce and eat quickly in a dark room. *(Looking off stage).* Where *is* Idle Jack? I think he must have been brought up on sloe gin. He's the laziest man I know. When he reads a book he goes out in the garden to read it, and waits for the wind to blow and turn over the pages for him. One night last week our house caught fire, but he wouldn't get out of bed until one of the firemen had brought him up a cup of tea. He never eats beef, he says it's too much trouble to reach for the mustard. I've known him to sit next to our old Tom cat for hours, then he purrs, the cat mistakes him for one of her kittens and starts to lick his face, that saves him the trouble of washing himself. I am sure when he dies he will be late for his funeral. Ah here he comes dashing along like a steamroller with a punctured tyre.

(Enter Idle Jack *slowly. He looks at cook and starts to gape.)*

So here you are. You must have been born on 'Lazy' Day. You are a nice sort of young man to bring a girl out for a picnic. And don't stand there gaping like a cod-fish. And stop that arguing. You *ought* to take a girl out, you did. You don't know how to take a dog for a walk.

Every time you go into a public house, you leave me outside. A nice way to treat me.

JACK: I haven't *treated* you at all yet.

ELIZA: Don't you think I've got a thirst as well as you—Oh, you give me the hump.

JACK: If you've got the hump you should be able to go without drink, like the other camels do.

ELIZA: Don't you call me a camel. Let me tell you my father was Mayor of Brighton.

JACK: If your father was a mare, you must be a foal.

ELIZA: How dare you, I'll scream.

JACK: If you scream then you *will* be a 'little horse.'

ELIZA: If I am a horse I want a *bit* in my mouth—where's the grub?

JACK: *(Handing her food tied up in handkerchief.)* Here's our banquet.

ELIZA: *(Looking in bundle.)* You've forgotten the salt—go back and get it.

JACK: I can't go all that way back, my legs aren't strong enough.

ELIZA: Call those legs—they are more like a couple of hairpins.

(She spreads out food on floor. They both sit.)

JACK: Where's that half an egg—here it is—is this the butter?

ELIZA: No, you fool, that's not butter, you've brought the soap.

JACK: So I have. Never mind, you know what the saying is, 'Where there's life there's *soap.*'

ELIZA: You mean, 'Where there's Life*buoy* there's soap.' *(Pointing to food.)* Look, there's a wasp

73

on that jam-tart! *(Jack puts his foot in it.)* Now see what you've done, fathead, you've done in our dinner.

JACK: *(Removing jam-tart from boot.)* Never mind, we'll shut our eyes when we eat it and think it's a trifle.

ELIZA: Your feet are no trifle. I'm too upset to eat now. When I saw you kill that wasp, my heart came up in my throat.

JACK: Well eat that, you like sheeps' hearts, don't you?

ELIZA: I know what we'll do, we'll have a vegetarian dinner.

JACK: How can we do that?

ELIZA: Let's run round the fields and nibble the grass. A few nettles would do you good, you silly ass.

JACK: Never mind about the food, let us sit and talk to the sunshine.

ELIZA: What is the good of talking to the sunshine when you are hungry?

JACK: Well, the sun is very good to *'eat.*

ELIZA: That *'eat* isn't what you eat—don't you know your geography yet?

JACK: Well, isn't *'ot, 'eat?*

ELIZA: But 'ot ain't the eat you eat with.

JACK: Who told you so?

ELIZA: Dick Whittington. He knows, he does. His father was a man of letters.

JACK: What—a postman? I don't like Dick, he's too swanky for me.

ELIZA: Yes, and what about that ugly little minx, Alice, she's in love with him.

JACK: Alice isn't bad looking. Of course, she's got a different kind of beauty to yours. Your face is more of the Gothic type, but when you get hot at cooking, then your face is more Grecian, in fact, it's all over grease.

ELIZA: I don't mind telling you I'm afraid of Dick. He has threatened to tell Fitzwarren that we bribed the milkman to give short weight, so that I could make you your tapioca puddings. What had we better do? Let me see, what's to-day?

JACK: *(Taking out watch.)* It's just half past three.

ELIZA.   I didn't ask you what the date was. *(Looking at watch.)* That's Fitzwarren's watch.

JACK: Well, I wanted to know the time.

ELIZA: Why didn't you take the egg-boiler then.

JACK: *(Catching sight of* Dick's *bundle, which he left by the milestone.)* Look, that bundle belongs to Dick. I recognise the stain on the corner.

ELIZA: Well, what's the bundle to do with you?

JACK: I've got an idea in my head.

ELIZA: That's the first time there's ever been anything in there.

JACK: Shush! Let us put the watch in Dick's bundle. Fitzwarren will recognise his *gilded* watch.

ELIZA: Then Dick and watch will both be *guilty*.

JACK: *(Putting watch in bundle.)* It will be safe in there away from this keen spring air.

ELIZA: You don't mean spring air, you mean 'air spring.

JACK: Now swear to secrecy.

ELIZA: I swear.

JACK: Don't swear out loud, the sparrows might hear

you. Now give the sign of the A. S. S.

ELIZA: What's the A. S. S.

JACK: The Ananias Secret Society.

ELIZA: Anna who? I've never heard of her.

(Both give signs to each other, by waving hands over head etc. Then shaking hands to seal their vow.)

(A short duet to be introduced here, or the following words can be used to the air of 'The Bogie Man.')

BOTH: Shush! Shush! Shush! We've hit upon a plan,
To have revenge on Dirty Dick and harm him all we can,
Shush! Shush! Shush! we'll thwart him in his prime,
And poor old Dick, just like the watch, will soon be doing time.

(They do a slow mysterious dance to same tune. After dance Eliza *and* Jack *exeunt.)*

Enter Fitzwarren

FITZ: Well, here I am on 'ighgate 'ill. Whenever I come to 'ighgate 'ill, *I get well.* I love to be in the country and sniff the ozone from the radish trees. There is nothing like deep breathing to *brace* me up. *(Takes deep breath—bang heard off stage.* Fitz *puts his hand inside his waistcoat, and pulls out a pair of broken braces.)* I should have said it 'braces me down.' Anyone got a piece of string—Perhaps the band will give me a *cord* on. Never mind, my clothes will keep up by their own reputation—they are made at my shop. What a shop! I sell everything from a pen'orth of peas to a piano. What a shop!

All the latest improvements. If you want to go to the second floor, you just stand on a sack of self-raising flour and up you go. If you happen to have an old braces-button, just bring it to my shop and I'll sew you a new pair of trousers on to it. With every pound of dog's biscuits I give you a dog. I keep the dogs in the drapery department, because they so often want *muslin*.

(Song to be introduced here or the following words may be used to the air of 'Come, Birdie, Come.'

SONG:

Come, people, come and shop from me,
I sell fine coffee, rice and tea,
Paper and string I give you free,
Come, people, come, and shop from me.

Come, people, come, and shop from me.
Sausages with a pedigree,
And tins of fresh sardines from the sea,
Come, people, come, and shop from me.

Come, people, come, and shop from me.
Honey and wax made by the bee,
I put all their stings into my tea,
Come, people, come, and shop from me.

Come, people, come, and shop from me.
I've excellent boots from off the tree,
With each I give a guarantee,
Come, people, come, and shop from me.

Come, people, come, and shop from me.
I've golf clubs in variety,
I sell you the caddy with the tee,
Come, people, come, and shop from me.

Come, people, come, and shop with me,
I've stockings made of sponge you see,
They are good if you've water on the knee.
Come, people, come, and shop with me.

(Enter Dick *and* Alice)

ALICE: Hullo Dad, I'm so upset.

77

FITZ:	Who spilt you?
ALICE:	I am upset because Dick is going away to sea.
FITZ:	Who is he going to *see*?
DICK:	No. I'm going to sea—see?
FITZ:	But I don't see. I'd better put my glasses on. What 'C' are you going to see?
DICK:	Why the big sea.
FITZ:	Oh, the capital C, I see.
DICK:	No. I mean the sea that goes up and down.
FITZ:	Oh, the sea *saw*.
DICK:	There will be no saw in this sea—the sea, see.
FITZ:	'C.C.'—Cissy—what's her other name?
DICK:	*(Embracing* Alice.) There is no other girl in the whole world for me but Alice.
FITZ:	Stop that—what are you doing—pressing your *suit*.
ALICE:	Don't be angry Dad, Dick loves me.
FITZ:	Well, Dick does seem a bit *mashed*—let's call him Dick-*tater*.
DICK:	I am leaving England sir, as soon as I can find a ship.
FITZ:	Court-*ship* seems to be the only ship you want.
DICK:	And when I return a rich man, I shall ask you for your daughter's hand.
FITZ:	If you want her hand you must take all of her. I don't sell my daughter in pen'orths.
ALICE:	But won't it be lovely, Dad, when Dick and I are wed.
FITZ:	What about me, who's going to make my gruel

78

and fill my hot water bottle?

DICK: Never mind sir, we will all be happy by and by.

(Trio to be introduced here, or the following may be sung to the air of 'There's a Tavern in the Town.')

DICK: There's a future waiting me—waiting me,
Out in a country 'cross the sea.

FITZ: Wait and see.

ALICE: And when you are so far away,
I vow I'll think of you each day,

DICK: Fare thee well for I must leave you,
Do not let this parting grieve you,

ALICE: Oh remember me when out in foreign parts—sweetheart,

DICK: Adieu,

ALICE: Adieu, Adieu, Adieu.

DICK: And soon I'll come back o'er the raging main,
And may we all soon meet again.

(All Exit. Re-enter Fitz.)

FITZ: *(Looking about stage as though seeking something)* I've lost my watch. I thought I was a little *out of time* in that song. I know I had it this morning because I remember timing the eggs with it. Now I don't know if it is half past two or Thursday week.

(Enter Jack and Eliza. They watch Fitz looking about stage.)

JACK: What are you looking for?

FITZ: I don't know, but I'll tell you when I've found it.

(All three stand in a line as they sing the following in style of burlesque opera. All the music re-

79

quired is a chord after each sentence.)

FITZ: A word allow me
Kind lady and gentleman,
I'm feeling sadly,
I want your help badly,
For I've lost my watch.

JACK: He's lost his watch,

COOK: His watch!

JACK: He's lost his watch!
Pray calm yourself—don't carry on,
Was your watch going?

FITZ: Yes, it was going—but now it's *gone.*

COOK: It's gone!

FITZ: It's gone!

COOK: It is our belief we know the thief.

JACK: The thief we know, sir.

FITZ: His name I say, come answer quick,

COOK: It's no other than young Dirty Dick,

FITZ: It cannot was—it cannot be,

JACK: Look in yon bundle and you'll see,

  (Fitz takes watch from bundle.)

FITZ: The watch I've found. Upon my soul,

COOK: Upon his soul,

JACK: His Inger*sole.*

  (Music stops.)

  (Enter Dick *and* Alice.)

FITZ: And so, Wick Dickington—er—Dick Whiting-
ton, you are a thief. You stole my watch.

80

DICK:	It is a lie. I am innocent.
ALICE:	Father, how can you say such a thing, my Dick could never steal.
JACK:	I like that. Why, I saw him steal a kiss from you just now, right under your very nose.
DICK:	This is some vile plot to ruin me. *(To* Fitz*)* You don't believe it, sir? *(Fitz turns up back of stage and shrugs his shoulders, as though sobbing. Dick then turns to* Eliza.*)* And you Eliza, you have known me all my life, since I was a baby. Do you think I could *rob* anyone?
ELIZA:	Well, you were brought up on *Robb's* biscuits and you always had such *taking* ways.
DICK:	*(To* Jack*)* Although we have not always been the best of friends, surely you think I am innocent?
JACK:	Perhaps you had a sudden attack of clocktermania, you know what that is, it means taking things and not knowing you are taking them. My father suffered from it. He often took the wrong turning when he came home on Saturday night, and he had no idea he had taken it until he woke next morning in the horse trough.
DICK:	Will no one believe that I am innocent?
ALICE:	Yes, Dick, *I will.* I swear you are innocent.
ELIZA:	A *real* lady never swears.
DICK:	*(To* Alice*)* Thank you, darling. I will yet prove my innocence to the whole world, and I will bring the guilty one face to face with justice.
	*(*Eliza *and* Jack *tremble at the knees.)*
ELIZA:	*(To* Jack*)* What are you shivering for—it isn't cold.
JACK:	I'm not shivering, but all my blood has gone jazzy. Look at yourself, you are wobbling like a plate of jellied eels with the bones taken out.

FITZ: Stop this prattle. The truth will yet be known. But let us think of happier things this lovely summer morning.

> Let's be joyful, let's be gay,
> Suppose we sing a little lay.

DICK: A good idea, for now's our chance,
To enjoy a little song and dance.

ELIZA: When ere I get to 'ighgate 'ill,
I find my legs will not keep still.

JACK: So let's join hands and have a fling,
And like the other birds, we'll sing.

(Concerted number. The following may be used to the air of 'Cold and Frosty Morning.')

ALL: Let's go down the Bull and Bush
The Bull and Bush, the Bull and Bush,
Let's go down to the Bull and Bush,
This lovely summer morning.
What shall we drink when we get there,
When we get there, when we get there,
We'll have a glass of vintage rare,
This lovely summer morning.
Which one of us is going to pay,
Going to pay, going to pay,
We'll toss, it's quite the fairest way,
This lovely summer morning.

JACK: I haven't got a single brown,

ELIZA: A single brown,

D.& A.   A single brown.

FITZ: I've only got this half-a-crown,
This lovely summer morning.

JACK: Well, toss it up for who's to pay,

ALL: Who's to pay, who's to pay,

DICK: Then heads or tails we'll quickly say,
This lovely summer morning.

(Fitz *tosses imaginary coin. A coin is heard to drop off stage. All on stage look for coin.)*

ELIZA: Now we cannot have a drink,

FITZ: Have a drink,

JACK: Have a drink,
For the coin has fallen down a sink,
On this lovely summer morning.

(All dance. All Exit. Alice re-enters.)

ALICE: Poor Dick. What a cruel shame to accuse him of doing such a wicked crime. He is too noble, too true to stoop so low. If there ever was a white man upon this earth his name is Dick Whittington. Never mind what others think, *I* love him with all my heart. He is all the world to me.

(Any love ballad can be sung here. Something of the 'My Hero' style of song. After song, exit Alice. Eliza enters from opposite side.)

ELIZA: That Jack is the limit. We have a meat jack at home with better manners than he has. He buys a bag of winkles and borrows my hair pin to pick them out with, and eats them all himself—all he gave me was a couple of the shells to have made up into a brooch. He always was a *shell-fish* lad. The only thing he ever gave me, was last winter, when he kissed me and gave me the 'flu. I was in bed for a week; he came to see me twice and then he pinched two of my grapes and a dose of my cod liver oil. He is the sort of man who would give his girl a clay pipe for her birthday present, and then expect her to buy the tobacco for him to smoke in it. That was a dirty trick he did with that watch. You see, the idea is, he wants to marry Alice, so that she can go to work while he stops at home and keeps the books. He should be able to keep books all right, his father was a bookmaker. Of course, I want Jack to marry me; if I don't get off soon I shall be ending my days in the remnant basket. If I don't get proposed to soon, I shall have to wait until Leap Year and propose to Fitzwarren, then I'll give him fits. If I don't get married I shall have to go on the stage and elope with a Duke, then I shall be a Duck. I should be a treasure to any man—he will only have to taste my peach smellba—that's the same as peach melba, only it's made with onions—then he will propose on the spot. Poets have written songs about my puddings, they would have written lots more but they couldn't rhyme 'tapioca.' This is a song a lover of mine wrote about the way I cooked kippers.

(Song. Air: 'Those Golden Slippers.')

Oh, those golden kippers,
Oh, those golden kippers,
Golden kippers, 'Liza cooked were very, very
    nice,
Oh, those golden kippers,
Oh, those golden kippers,
They were all so high they made me think of
    Paradise.

(Music repeats while Eliza *dances round stage.* Dick *enters.)*

DICK: What *are* you doing?

ELIZA: I'm on a cook's excursion.

DICK: I am too sad to be frivolous. I've been accused of dishonesty. I must and *will* get this stain from off my good name.

ELIZA: Well, try a little Vim, it removes all stains.

DICK: Stop this jesting, Eliza. Think, what will become of me if the world thinks I'm a thief?

84

ELIZA:	Don't worry, they'll make you a company promoter.
DICK:	I wonder who could have put that watch in my knapsack?
ELIZA:	Perhaps the watch got run down and ran in by itself.
DICK:	Supposing I get into the arms of the law?
ELIZA:	I've often been in the arms of the law.
DICK:	You have?
ELIZA:	Yes, two strong arms of the law, when I've been squeezed by my favourite policeman.
DICK:	Ah! perhaps he could help me out of my dilemma.
ELIZA:	I don't think he cares for lemons.
DICK:	Is he a man of intellect—is he sharp?
ELIZA:	He must be *sharp,* he's always on *point* duty. I've seen the point.
DICK:	He may be able to tell me what steps I should take.
ELIZA:	I expect he will tell you to take *long* steps and run away. I'll introduce you to him; he is on duty now round the corner.
DICK:	What is he doing?
ELIZA:	He is watching a gas meter, in case it escapes. *(Exeunt Dick and Eliza. Enter Alice from opposite side.)*
ALICE:	What will poor Dick do, I wonder. I must find him and give him some word of hope.
	(Jack enters and quickly kneels before Alice.)
JACK:	Behold, your loving Jack—upon my knees I sit,

85

Just gaze at my position, quite un-knee-sy
    you'll admit,
Say the word that you'll be mine, give me your
    answer quick,
I'm Jack,you Queen, we want the King, then we
    can do the trick.

ALICE: How dare you make love to me! I hate the sight
of you.

JACK: Well, marry me with your eyes shut. *He drops
his head as he continues,* Alice *run off.* Cook
re-enters quickly, taking the place of Alice. *This
is all unnoticed by* Jack, *he continues as though
he was still addressing* Alice.)

I love your pretty face. I worship every dimple.
Your big blue eyes are like the skies,
They each shine like a star,
Your dainty feet so trim and neat,
They are! They are! They are!

ELIZA: *(Speaking in an artificial voice.)* But what will
your Eliza say?

JACK: Sh! She's got a face like a fried egg that has
been run over.

ELIZA: What?

JACK: *(Looks up and discovers his mistake.)* Good
Heavens, I've revoked.

ELIZA: So that's what you think of me is it? You under-
sized son of a slug. I see your plans now. You
wanted to get Dick out of the way so that you
might marry Alice.

JACK: It's all right, cookie.

ELIZA: It's all *wrong* cookie. I'll confess all, you grov-
elling grasshopper. I'll tell Fitzwarren the
truth.

(Enter Fitzwarren*)*

86

FITZ:	You'll tell me *what?*
JACK:	*(To* Eliza*)* Don't! Don't! I'll give you all my cigarette cards and half my cricket bat if you don't tell.
FITZ:	What does all this mean?
JACK:	*(To* Fitz*)* I don't know what she is going to say, but it isn't true if she does say it.
FITZ:	Explain! What do you *mean* Jack?
ELIZA:	Yes 'mean Jack' is right. You *are* a mean Jack. You know Dick is innocent. *You* made me put that watch in Dick's bundle.
FITZ:	I can't believe my own ears.
JACK:	Have one of mine.
ELIZA:	It is true, sir. And after I did all that for him he wants to jolt—er—jilt me.
FITZ:	So all this means but one thing. It means that Dick is innocent.

*(*Dick *and* Alice *enter)*

ALICE:	Oh, father, what words of joy.
FITZ:	*(Offering hand to* Dick.*)* Will you forgive me Dick?
DICK:	Indeed I will, sir.

I want you, sir, to understand
I don't bear any malice,
But now command the dainty hand
Of your fair daughter, Alice.

FITZ:	She is yours my boy. Bless you my children.
ELIZA:	Now, Master Dick, you've done the trick. We both congratulate you.
DICK:	You run away without delay Or I shall spiflicate you. *(Shakes fist*

at Eliza *and* Jack.*)*

ALICE: Dear Dick, you're right, but do not fight,
For our pantomime's just ended,
They'll make amends, let's all be friends,
What say you, father?

FITZ: Splendid!
Let this be said, my cook must wed,
For long years she was waited,
So, Jack, you cur, you marry her.

JACK: I'd rather be cremated.

DICK: More church bells chime you'll hear when I'm
Wedded to my Alice,
My lot she'll share when I'm Lord Mayor
And live within a palace.

FINALE

*(The final number should be a bright song of the
moment. Something popular. It should, if possible,
be one to fit in the latest dance)*

SINDBAD,

The Salt Sea Sailor

(1928)

CHARACTERS:
Sindbad.
Old Man of the Sea.
Mrs. Sindbad.
Captain Spanker.
Princess.

SCENE: The Island of Balsora. Lights down.
Mysterious music.

Enter Old Man of the Sea. He should be
dressed in green tights. Long flowing hair
and beard.

OLD MAN: Don't be afraid, I'll harm you not, so have no
    fear of me,
I'm simply known as Undumic—the old man of
    the sea.
I once was young and handsome, but now I'm
    old and weird,
My ears have turned to cockle-shells—I've
    seaweed for my beard.
The mermaids used to love me once, but now
    they pass me by,
They have no time for things like me—they've
    other fish to fry.
These mermaids used to romp with me beneath
    the perm'nent wave,
But now they like the shingle best, since they
    have learnt to shave.
At night when I'm feeling tired and want to rest
    my bones,

I have to seek some quiet cave, along with Davy
   Jones.
We borrow Father Neptune's crown and some
   ship's anchor too,
And we play at crown and anchor the whole
   long evening through.
I'm here to guard the precious stones, hidden
   on the shore,
The merchants from the outer world have eyes
   upon my store.
There's one brave sailor, Sindbad, who comes
   from other climes,
These treasures he's been seeking now for nigh
   on twenty times.
Each voyage he vows will be his last, and yet he
   comes again;
I almost think it's time he was rewarded for his
   pain.
This morn I fancied I espied a strange craft out
   at sea,
The kind of craft that Sindbad sails, perchance
   it may be he.
I'll hie myself back to my cave and watch from
   out the crack,
And if I see some stranger here I'll soon be on
   his track,
So fare thee well, 'Twill not be long before we
   meet again,
I fear I cannot do a dance, my limbs won't
   stand the strain,
But after all I can but try although I'm old and
   weak,
With joy I often *bubble,* and my joints they always *squeak.*

(He does a short dance to music of 'The March
of the Marionettes.' He is very slow with his
steps. The effect of squeaking joints can be done
off stage, by means of a wooden rattle. Exit after dance. Lights up.)

   Enter Mrs. Sindbad.

90

(She has a life-belt round her neck. A pair of water-wings in her hand. Small spade and pail, etc.)

MRS. SINDBAD: Oh what a tripe—er—trip! I've nearly lost my eyesight looking for land. I got a bit of grit in my eye twice, and that's the only bit of land I've seen for a week. I don't wonder that Nelson lost his eye when at sea. We lost our way three times. It's so awkward when you are on a ship, having to get out of your warm bed and knocking up a lighthouse to ask them the way. Mr. Eddystone got most annoyed when we called on him last Thursday. You see, it was his early closing day and he didn't like it. I climbed up the rock and knocked at his front door. Mr. Eddystone was upstairs at the time having a bit of 'shut eye' I fancy—I think he called it a 'siesta'—but I didn't wait to see Esther. When he heard me knocking he looked out of his top window, and they *are* top windows in lighthouses. Well, he looked down at me and I looked up at him—he did look a long way away—I looked as high as I could look and he looked as low as he could look, and then our looks only just met. We couldn't hear a word each other said, we might have been speaking shorthand—his mouth was going like this *(Business of rapidly moving lips without saying a word)* and my mouth kept on going like this *(Same business as before)* and that was all we said to each other. After we had had about half an hour's conversation like that he dropped me down a piece of paper wrapped round a stone—it wasn't really a stone, but his name being Eddy*stone* he used half his name. When I picked up this piece of paper it had written on it 'One large white and a small brown'—you see, he must have thought I was the baker. He then went in and shut the window and I came away. You do feel so silly when you're lost at sea—you can't tell one wave from another. You never know which is the High Street. Why they

91

can't have a few floating signposts I can't understand, or a few water policemen swimming about. Let those who want the sea have it—it's no good to me. I'd rather be on terra-cotta all the time.

(Here a comic song to be introduced or the following can be used to the air of 'Nancy Lee.')

If on the sea you're asked to go,
Don't go, my lads! Oh don't go—Oh no,
That's where the stormy winds do blow,
They blow—what Oh—they blow.
Once on the main I get a pain right in my neck,
If sea is rough, I have enough, I feel a wreck,
When tempests blow I go below, I leave the deck,
Below I just *heave* O!

Chorus
A sailor's life is not the life for me,
Oh no! Oh no! I hate the sea;
The sailor's say a sailor's life is *free*.
And that's all that it is worth to me.

Repeat Choruses
A sailor's life is not the life for me,
Oh no! Oh no! I hate the sea,
A sailor always calls his ship a 'she,'
They'll never make a ship of me.

A sailor's life is not the life for me,
Oh no! Oh no! I hate the sea,
I'd rather wed a jolly old bargee,
With sailors you are all at sea.

(Short dance at end of song.)

(Enter Sindbad *dressed as sailor. Small hat, etc.)*

SINDBAD: I say, Mother, I do wish you'd be a bit more careful—do you know what you did?

MRS. SINDBAD: What did I did?

SINDBAD: Why, you came out of the ship and forgot to shut the street door.

MRS. SINDBAD: Well, what *of* it?

SINDBAD: Well a shark has got in and swallowed the umbrella stand.

MRS. SINDBAD: Did he now? It says in Old Moore's Almanack that if a shark swallows an umbrella stand it's a sign of rain.

SINDBAD: We are going to have some rain right enough—my corns have been shooting.

MRS. SINDBAD: I know your corns have been shooting—they've shot some nice big holes in your socks too—I say *darn* the things.

SINDBAD: The last pair of my socks that you darned you left the needle in the heel.

MRS. SINDBAD: Well, what *of* it?

SINDBAD: Well, I got the pins and needles every time I walked.

MRS. SINDBAD: Never mind about that—is the ship all right?

SINDBAD: Yes, I've tied it up to a lamp-post.

MRS. SINDBAD: I hope it won't get burnt, it will then become a light ship.

SINDBAD: Well, we've already *alighted,* haven't we?

MRS. SINDBAD: Now are you sure this is the island where the treasures are?

SINDBAD: Of course it is—haven't I been here before?

MRS. SINDBAD: Well, what *of* it?

SINDBAD: But, Mother, this is my fourth visit to the Treasure Island.

MRS. SINDBAD: Well, I know that you have been always pop-

93

ping off to these foreign parts; I wonder you don't have a season ticket.

SINDBAD: Do you remember my first trip, when I thought I had found an island and really it was the back of a whale?

MRS. SINDBAD: That tale always sounded a bit 'fishy' to me.

SINDBAD: But it was true, Mother. As soon as I 'backed' that whale he ran away.

MRS. SINDBAD: Ah, those sort of *whales* are called 'welshers' I think.

SINDBAD: Well, anyhow it made me 'wail' a bit when I had to swim for my life.

MRS. SINDBAD: I know, but if you had met a shark you would have been well 'down in the mouth.' I don't hold with all this gadding about the world.

SINDBAD: But, Mother, you know I was born to live on the water.

MRS. SINDBAD: Well, why don't you stop at home and be a plumber?

SINDBAD: You don't seem to understand, Mother, if I get hold of some of these treasures we shall be ever so rich.

MRS. SINDBAD: Well, what *of* it?

SINDBAD: Wouldn't you like to have everything rich?

MRS. SINDBAD: No—I'm sure they'd make me bilious.

SINDBAD: It only means finding the right spot, and we shall pick up precious stones as big as coconuts.

(A siren whistle is heard off-stage.)

MRS. SINDBAD: *(Looking up.)* It sounds a bit windy under-foot—doesn't it?

SINDBAD: *(Looking up.)* Oh, Mother! That is the giant roc bird—he is a bird of prey.

94

MRS. SINDBAD: A bird of prey—well I do wish he'd say his prayers a little quieter.

(A coconut falls on stage.)

SINDBAD: *(Picking up nut.)* Look what was dropped by the roc bird.

MRS. SINDBAD: What is it—a *rock* cake?

SINDBAD: Don't be silly, Mother—this is a coconut.

MRS. SINDBAD: Well, what *of* it?

SINDBAD: A coconut.

MRS. SINDBAD: *(Indicating head.)* Yes, it nearly fell on *mine*. It is no good you trying to tell me roc birds lay coconuts instead of eggs.

SINDBAD: The bird didn't lay it—he was carrying it in his claws and dropped it.

MRS. SINDBAD: Serve it right—it should carry a string bag.

SINDBAD: This bird was taking it home to feed its young.

MRS. SINDBAD: There's a nice sort of Mother for you. Fancy giving its children coconut to eat before they are short-coated.

SINDBAD: But they are *wild* birds.

MRS. SINDBAD: No wonder they are wild if they have coconuts to eat—it's enough to make any baby get wild.

SINDBAD: But these birds are so strong they can eat anything.

MRS. SINDBAD: Ah well, I suppose they can do as they like with their own gizzards.

SINDBAD: Do you know these birds could swoop down and carry *you* off?

MRS. SINDBAD: Well, what *of* it?

SINDBAD: Do you mean to say you wouldn't mind being carried off by a giant bird?

95

MRS. SINDBAD: *(Getting frightened.)* Don't be silly 'Sinny'—do you mean to say one of those birds could carry *me*?

SINDBAD: Of course they could.

MRS. SINDBAD: If they come here and start messing me about I shall shish 'em off quick.

SINDBAD: They wouldn't be afraid of you—why they'd—

(A large red lump is thrown on from side of stage. This is to represent a piece of raw meat. It has several large pieces of coloured glass concealed inside it.)

MRS. SINDBAD: *(Jumping with fright).* What's that?

SINDBAD: Ah, a lump of raw meat.

MRS. SINDBAD: Now, you are not going to tell me that bullocks are flying about here in the air?

SINDBAD: No—I'll tell you what this is.

MRS. SINDBAD: *(Examining meat).* I know what it is—it's a bit of shin of beef, and if it had been cut a bit lower it would have been cow-heel.

SINDBAD: Listen, Mother. This is a piece of raw meat that has been thrown down from the side of the Silver Mountain.

MRS. SINDBAD: Oh, it's silverside.

SINDBAD: No. It has been thrown down the mountain side by some merchants who are too frightened to venture nearer.

MRS. SINDBAD: Why are they throwing their meat away—have they all turned vegetarians?

SINDBAD: No. You see, as the meat rolls down the mountain side, the precious stones lying about stick to the meat.

MRS. SINDBAD: Well, what *of* it?

SINDBAD: Well, then the stones are in the meat.

MRS. SINDBAD: They always sell meat by the *stone*.

SINDBAD: See—the stones have already stuck to the meat.

MRS. SINDBAD: Well, let us stick to the stones.

SINDBAD: The idea is this: The merchants at the top of the mountain know that the raw meat will gather the precious stones, and soon the roc bird will see the meat and carry it off to its lair.

MRS. SINDBAD: You mean its larder.

SINDBAD: When the bird reaches its lair with the meat, all covered with precious stones, the merchants frighten the bird away and collect the stones from off the meat.

MRS. SINDBAD: That's a good idea—it's the same as a mouse trap, but it's done with meat.

SINDBAD: Ah, I have an idea.

MRS. SINDBAD: You have two *eyes dear*.

SINDBAD: Let us take the precious stones sticking to the meat before the bird gets it. *(He takes out the pieces of glass concealed in the 'meat')*. Won't the merchants be surprised when they find the meat is stoneless?

MRS. SINDBAD: Yes, they'll think it's a Sunmaid Raisin.

(Both proceed to take out pieces of coloured glass).

MRS. SINDBAD: *(Chuckling to herself)*. This is a bit of luck *(Shows a large piece of green glass)*. Look at this lovely Hammersmith.

SINDBAD: *(With two pieces of glass)*. And these two diamonds.

MRS. SINDBAD: I wonder if we can find the ace?

SINDBAD: Look here, Mother. *(Shows her handful of stones)*. They are worth millions.

97

MRS. SINDBAD: Won't they make a lovely rockery for the drawing-room.

(Siren whistle heard off).

MRS. SINDBAD: There goes the hooter—it must be one o'clock.

SINDBAD: No, Mother—it's the roc bird!

MRS. SINDBAD: Well, what *of* it?

SINDBAD: Don't let him see the meat—he may swoop down here and carry us away. Cover up the meat quick, before he sees it.

(Siren whistle heard off).

SINDBAD: How can we disguise it?

MRS. SINDBAD: I know—make a noise like a fish and he'll think it's a red herring.

(Whistle off).

SINDBAD: Quick, it's coming nearer. What *is* to be done?

MRS. SINDBAD: Put a big of salt on its tail—a bit of 'roc' salt.

SINDBAD: The bird must not see that meat.

MRS. SINDBAD: Well, I hope you don't expect me to *eat* it.

SINDBAD: No, but we must make it look like something else.

MRS. SINDBAD: I know—I'll sit on it and it will then look like a sandwich. *(She sits on 'meat'—as she does so they both gaze up above as though watching the flight of the bird).* Is he looking?

SINDBAD: I can't see the 'birdseye.'

MRS. SINDBAD: He's too 'shaggy' for 'birdseye'. I should like to give his neck a 'thick twist.' I suppose those birds have 'Wills' of their own. Well, *I* hope he goes away and we get no 'returns.'

(Sound of whistle dying away in distance).

SINDBAD: I think he has gone.

MRS. SINDBAD: Well, what *of* it?

SINDBAD: Now, Mother, we must get to work and collect the precious stones.

MRS. SINDBAD: But, Sindbad dear, before we start
Let's sing a song to cheer our heart.

SINDBAD: But, Mother, use your voice with care
For you know it's rather the worse for wear.

MRS. SINDBAD: Well, what *of* it?

(Here a duet between Sindbad *and* Mrs. Sindbad *to be introduced. The following can be used. Air—'The Vicar of Bray.')*

SINDBAD: Now, Mother, we must both work hard to find the hidden treasure,
For then we both shall be so rich and live a life of leisure.

MRS. SINDBAD: What do you want with precious stones? You've got a wealthy uncle,
Who has a very ruby nose also a big carbuncle.

SINDBAD: But think how we shall be repaid when we have done our labours,
We can take the jewels home with us and show them to the neighbours.
P'raps we can sell them to the King: from him we'd get our *full*worth,

MRS. SINDBAD: Or if the King won't buy them we can then try Mr. Woolworth.

SINDBAD: You can put a ruby in your hat and go and see Aunt Millie,

MRS. SINDBAD: And p'raps a diamond on my nose if the weather should be chilly.

SINDBAD: I'll give my girls long strings of pearls and one for Uncle Charlie,

MRS. SINDBAD: And if we get too many pearls we'll use them as
pearl barley.

SINDBAD: There're lots of sapphires here I'm told, they
grow among the nettle,

MRS. SINDBAD: A sap-*phire* would be nice at home on which to
boil the kettle.

SINDBAD: To carry all our precious stones we'll want a
cart and pony.

MRS. SINDBAD: But even then we shan't be rich—we're bound
to go home *stoney*.

(After duet, Mrs. Sindbad *goes off.* Sindbad *remains. Enter* Old Man of the Sea).

OLD MAN: What's this upon the island? A man I do
perceive
It is the sailor Sindbad, unless my eyes deceive.

SINDBAD: *(Slightly nervous).* Yes, Undumic, here I am
again—d—d—don't be frightened, I shan't
hurt you.

OLD MAN: Such men as you could not harm me, on human
beings I thrive,
Why, in my time I've eaten men as big as you
alive.

SINDBAD: Y—y—yes I know, but don't you eat me because I come from a very indigestible family.

OLD MAN: Oh fear me not, I'll not harm you, all help I'll
gladly lend
For while you on this island stay, just count me
as your friend.

SINDBAD: That's very nice of you. I'll put in a word for
you to the manager of the MacFisheries. What's
happened in the old island since I was here last?
Have you gone in for greyhound racing yet?

OLD MAN: Since last you on this island came, cruel death
has left its sting;

	The hand of fate ordained it and took our precious King.
SINDBAD:	Good gracious, you don't mean to say King Wulla is dead. I *am* sorry. I made him a Frothblower on my last visit. He was a nice chap—I suppose he didn't say anything about me before he hopped it?
OLD MAN:	He spoke of you before he died, and said by his command, His greatest treasure you should have—the greatest in the land.
SINDBAD:	You don't mean to say the King has left me his goat.
OLD MAN:	Much rarer than the royal goat on you he has bestowed. The greatest treasure we possess is now yours—
SINDBAD:	Well I'm blowed. What is it like? Is it a ticket in the Calcutta Sweep or a couple of crocodiles?
OLD MAN:	He left to you his sweet Princess, whom everyone adores, On condition that you marry her this treasure island's yours; A precious gem of brilliant hue he placed within my care, See here it is *(Shows gem—in the shape of a heart)* such gems are very rare. 'That stone shall win my daughter's hand,' our noble King he said, So give this stone to our Princess, and henceforth you are wed.
SINDBAD:	That was a jolly good idea of poor old Kingy. I hope mother will like the Princess. I suppose I shall have to be introduced to my wife before I marry her—you can't have a wife you don't know, although mother always said it took her years before she knew father *(Making himself*

look smart by smoothing his hair, etc). I say, you might take me to where the Princess lives—all the caves are so much alike on this island, I don't know which is the royal cave.

OLD MAN: I'll take you to your dear Princess—her home it is afar,
But the way is long and hilly, and my legs won't stand the jar.

SINDBAD: It's no good talking like that—we can't take a tram, you haven't got any here.

OLD MAN: The journey must and shall be done to see your future bride,
But on your manly shoulders I shall have to surely ride.

SINDBAD: You are much too old ⸕ pick-a- backs —besides you are—

OLD MAN: If you refuse to carry me—then I must now away,
If you ignore our King's last wish, you'll live to rue the day.

SINDBAD: All right, I suppose I must carry you, but if you break my back in halves you'll have to mend it again. There's no one here to give you a bunk up, is there? (Old Man *gets on* Sindbad's *back*). We do look silly playing at 'horses.'

OLD MAN: Go journey on through yonder glade, around that cactus tree,
And very soon the beauteous face of your Princess you'll see,
Aud when you both meet face to face true love will fill your souls.

SINDBAD: When she sees you on my back, she'll think I've brought the coals.

(Exit R).

(Enter Captain Spanker *L).*

(He is a typical sea-faring man of the hale and hearty type. He dances on with folded arms, to the music of 'The Sailor's Hornpipe' and sings the following words to the same melody).

Let us shout hurray for the Captain bright and gay;
I am only happy when I'm on the sea,
For I cause a big commotion when I sail the mighty ocean,
We are very very happy in the King's Nav*ee*
Though our duty in the Navy is to do or die,
We are always bright and breezy and we're far from shy,
For my name is Captain Spanker, I'm a swanker when at anchor,
And I'm looking for a girlie with a downcast eye.

(Enter Mrs. Sindbad).

MRS. SINDBAD: Was that somebody asking for me? *(Droops her eyes and looks coy).*

CAPTAIN: Oh shiver me timbers, if it isn't Mrs. Sindbad.

MRS. SINDBAD: Well, what *of* it?

CAPTAIN: But it is Mrs. Sindbad, isn't it?

MRS. SINDBAD: Yes, I'm Mrs. Sindbad for the time being, but the name can soon be changed of course.

CAPTAIN: I think I'll change my course and steer the other way. We say in the Navy that widows are more dangerous than rocks, if you want to wreck your life.

MRS. SINDBAD: I thought I heard you say you were looking for someone with a downcast eye—won't I do?

CAPTAIN: But your eye only has a *cast* and no 'down.'

MRS. SINDBAD: Do you know, I'm awfully fond of sailors, and I always have Skipper's Sardines for tea. But you sailors are such naughty boys. *(Gives him a coy slap).*

CAPTAIN: Don't you believe it—we *tars* are not as black as we are painted.

MRS. SINDBAD: I suppose they call you *tars* because you can *pitch* such a good tale?

CAPTAIN: I don't know about that, but we have to keep our weather eye open—we never know when we are going to sight a little craft. *(Touches her under chin).*

MRS. SINDBAD: *(Giggling).* Oh, give hover. You are so like my fourth husband.

CAPTAIN: Was he a seafaring man?

MRS. SINDBAD: Oh yes—he used to guide the horse along the banks of the canal.

CAPTAIN: Was he Sindbad's father?

MRS. SINDBAD: No, he was the son of my fifth husband—that's why I called him Sin Bad, I put the 'D' in to make it look more even.

CAPTAIN: Let us sit here and talk of old times.

MRS. SINDBAD: Yes, do sit down—it saves wearing out our boots.

(They sit on tree stump up-stage).

CAPTAIN: I hope your Sindbad won't find us alone; he mightn't like it.

MRS. SINDBAD: He wouldn't mind, another step-father or two wouldn't worry him. He's used to 'em. Everytime he came home from a voyage and found a strange man about the house he called him 'Dad,' but once he came home when I had the bailiffs in and he called them *all* Father—it made me look so silly.

CAPTAIN: Never mind about the past—let us talk of the future.

MRS. SINDBAD: Oh! it's so romantic sitting here.

CAPTAIN: Ah! do you know what is above us?

MRS. SINDBAD: I know—that horrible almond rock bird.

CAPTAIN: No, I mean do you know what this tree is overhead?

MRS. SINDBAD: Well it looks like a Christmas tree with all the bon-bons cut off.

CAPTAIN: No. This is what is known as the Tree of Truth.

MRS. SINDBAD: Go on, I'll buy it—what do I have to say?

CAPTAIN: This is supposed to be a wonderful tree, according to the natives on this island. They say that anyone who tells a lie while under this tree will get a coconut on his head.

MRS. SINDBAD: That sounds jolly. I've got nothing to fear—I've never told a lie in the whole of my life.

(Coconut falls from above).

CAPTAIN: How do you account for that?

MRS. SINDBAD: I expect the tree is moulting.

CAPTAIN: Take no notice. I don't believe in it anyhow. Come to my arms. *(He embraces her).*

MRS. SINDBAD: Oh you flirt—what will your wife say?

CAPTAIN: Wife! I haven't got a wife.

(Coconut falls from above).

MRS. SINDBAD: Look at that! Your wife has called.

CAPTAIN: Nonsense! It's only a coincidence.

MRS. SINDBAD: It is not a coincidence—it's a coconut. Never mind, take no notice of the silly tree. If you are single, do you think you could learn to love me?

CAPTAIN: *(Looking up at tree as though expecting a coconut to fall).* Y— —ye—yes, I think I could.

MRS. SINDBAD: Oh, this is so sudden—how my girlish heart 'palps.' You know I am but a child still.

105

CAPTAIN: I can see that. If it is not a rude question, might I ask your age?

MRS. SINDBAD: I was twenty-two last Friday.

(A dozen or two coconuts fall from above. Mrs. Sindbad jumps up and makes towards exit).

CAPTAIN: Where are you going?

MRS. SINDBAD: I'm going to have this silly tree cut down.

CAPTAIN: Ah well! We sailors meet some queer fish in our travels. But we never get downhearted whatever we meet.

(Here the Captain might sing one of the numerous baritone songs regarding the sea. After song he goes off R. Princess enters L).

PRINCESS: Why must I live solitude and spend my days alone,
               While my poor heart is aching for someone to call my own,
               Here on this lonely island with the blue skies up above,
               The soft breezes whisper through the trees and seem to speak of love,
               If only I could meet my fate upon this lonely shore,
               My life would just be heaven—then I'd crave for nothing more.

(Here the Princess might sing any love ballad. After the song Mrs. Sindbad enters and looks at the Princess in surprise).

MRS. SINDBAD: Oh! a lady of the female sex. *(To Princess).* Excuse me, but could you direct me to the bargain basement?

PRINCESS: I do not understand. But tell me, who are you?

MRS. SINDBAD: Well, if it comes to that, who are you?

PRINCESS: I am a princess.

106

MRS. SINDBAD: A print dress?

PRINCESS: I am the Royal Princess. My late father was King of this island.

MRS. SINDBAD: Well I never did *(Bows to her)*. Pleased to meet you, your Royal *Harness,* and may you always have long *reins*—when will be your *bridle* day?

PRINCESS: That I do not know—alas!

MRS. SINDBAD: You don't want to know *a lass*—you want to know a *lad.* I suppose you haven't many young 'nuts' on this island.

PRINCESS: Nuts! Only coconuts.

MRS. SINDBAD: I don't mean nuts who drink cocoa. I mean those nuts that prefer the juice of the grape, with a little soda in it.

PRINCESS: I have no one here to love me.

MRS. SINDBAD: Well what *of* it—neither have I. But, bless you when I was your age I used to have my lovers queuing up at our back door all the evening.

PRINCESS: All things are so different here.

MRS. SINDBAD: Of course they are—it's certainly much quieter here than it is in Peckham Rye.

PRINCESS: If I could but find a lover I would lay my heart at his feet.

MRS. SINDBAD: I shouldn't do that—he might tread on it, and then you *would* die of a broken heart.

PRINCESS: When my father, the King, died he assured me that one day a handsome youth would arrive from over the seas and claim me for his bride.

MRS. SINDBAD: Well, don't lose heart—perhaps he's missed the boat. Of course, there is a big shortage of men just now, so if you do see one snap him up quick, that's my motto.

107

PRINCESS: It is the man who has the fellow gem to this *(Shows* Mrs. Sindbad *a heart-shaped gem which is attached to a cord she is wearing round her neck)* that is to be my husband.

MRS. SINDBAD: It looks like a bit of red currant jelly to me.

PRINCESS: Alas, it seems that he will never come.

MRS. SINDBAD: He'll turn up one of these days when you least expect him. He'll most likely come along some morning when you've got your hair in curl—I remember when I was courting my Horace—

(Sindbad enters with Old Man *on his back.* Mrs. Sindbad *turns and sees them.* Old Man *points to* Princess. Old Man *gets off* Sindbad's *shoulder and indicates that he shall go to the* Princess. Mrs. Sindbad *is confused, but continues her conversation to* Princess).

MRS. SINDBAD: As I was saying—when my Horace called and I was doing a bit of washing, with my ears all full of suds *(Sindbad pushes his mother away)*. Sinny! Sinny! what are you doing? *(To him in undertone)*. You musn't speak to her she's a— —

SINDBAD: Hush! *(He slowly advances towards* Princess *and shows her the gem he holds in his hand.* Princess *turns and takes off the cord round her neck—this she holds up in front of* Sindbad. Mrs. Sindbad *looks on in surprise)*.

MRS. SINDBAD: What are they doing—playing conkers?

(Old Man salaams and goes off).

PRINCESS: *(With extended arms towards* Sindbad*)*. My beautiful man.

MRS. SINDBAD: Well, I never did.

SINDBAD: Princess! *(They embrace)*. This is my mother.

PRINCESS: It can't be.

MRS. SINDBAD: Well, what *of* it? Sinny, put her down at once or you'll break her, and I can't afford to buy new princesses.

SINDBAD: Mother! I have met my fate.

MRS. SINDBAD: You wait till the park keeper sees you, there'll be a row. But what does all this mean?

PRINCESS: It means that your son holds the duplicate gem. *(Shows gem).* It was my father's wish that whoever found that gem I should wed.

SINDBAD: My future wife.

MRS. SINDBAD: I'd better go and have a look for some lucky stones—but I bet the only stone I shall find is a bit of hearthstone. *(Exit).*

SINDBAD: This—my darling—is the happiest moment in my life.

PRINCESS: And mine.

SINDBAD: It all seems too good to be true.
(The sound of singing birds is heard in the distance).

PRINCESS: Why, even the birds seem to be sharing our joy. They are trying to tell us what our future lives will be, when we live in our crystal cave facing the Sunny River.

(Any love duet can be introduced here, or the following may be used to the air of 'The Swanee River').

SINDBAD: Come down beside the Sunny River, there let us stray,
That's where I want to life for ever—that's where I want to stay.

PRINCESS: Our lives we now can spend together, ne'er shall we roam,
All through the bright and sunny weather here in my island home.

109

Refrain.

BOTH: All the world is gay and brighter, life's like paradise,
Oh darling how my heart grows lighter now I have won my prize.

(They exit arm in arm singing repeat refrain in harmony).

(Captain enters)

CAPTAIN: Well, all seems to be going well. I see Sindbad has made a match of it with the Princess. This means that he will have untold wealth, so I had better marry his mother then I shall come in for a bit of it. Ah! here comes Mrs. Sindbad *(Looking off)*. Good Heaven's, what has she been doing to herself?

(Enter Mrs. Sindbad with floral wreath round her head and dressed as an Arcadian).

CAPTAIN: Why! you look like a fruit salad.

MRS. SINDBAD: Well, what *of* it? This is the latest fashion according to the dressmakers on the island. I must make myself look a bit smart for Sindbad's wedding this afternoon.

CAPTAIN: Why not make a double wedding?

MRS. SINDBAD: *(Throwing herself into his arms)*. I'm yours for keeps.

CAPTAIN: But who can we find for our best man?

MRS. SINDBAD: How about the Old Man of the Sea—ah, here he is.

(Old Man enters with short hair and beard).

MRS. SINDBAD: Why, he's been shingled.

(Enter Sindbad and Princess).

110

OLD MAN: All happiness shall reign to-day.
             And every joy be ours,
             The nymphs upon their pipes shall play
             Within their leafy bowers.

             (Soft music is heard in the distance to be played
             till end of pantomime).

MRS. SINDBAD: And I have found another mate—
             A sea mate from the briny,
             He will make my number eight
             Come kiss your little 'Tiny.'

CAPTAIN: Now I am yours and you are mine
             You really are a wonder,
             I expect you'll find a number nine
             When I am put down under.

SINDBAD: And here upon this treasure isle
             I've got my fullest measure,
             And so now after all this while
             I've found my greatest treasure.

PRINCESS: I too have found a treasure rare;
             I'll never seek another,
             My Sindbad is beyond compare
             Also his darling mother.

             *(*Mrs. Sindbad *gives a low bow and falls over)*

                         Finale

             (Any bright popular song may be used here or
             the following may be substituted).

             Air —'Should auld acquaintance be forgot.'

ALL: Thus ends the happy Sindbad plot
             As told in pantomime,
             We hope we too have given you
             A really right good time.
             A very happy time to all
             A very happy time,
             Let voices ring and loudly sing
             For the Sindbad pantomime.

                                              111

BLUEBEARD

BOBBED

(1928)

CHARACTERS:
Bluebeard
Fatima
Anne
Toby
The Captain

SCENE: By Bluebeard's Palace.

MUSIC TO OPEN: Anything bright and
lively.

(Anne *enters.*)

ANNE: (*Hops round stage as she enters with a number
of parcels in her hands. Suddenly catches sight
of audience.*) Oh, there you are! I hope you'll
excuse me looking a bit higgledy-piggledy, but
I've just been doing a bit of shopping at the
sales, and I fancy I've caught a cold in the bargain basement. I've been hopping about like a
toad-in-the-hole. I started off in the millinery,
lost my hat so I went in the dresses, got pushed
out of that and found myself in the stockings,
then I lost my bearings and found myself in the
underwear. If I had stopped much longer I
should have found myself in the bearskin department, and then I should have found myself
in prison. So I took a seat on the cash railway
and came out before they pushed me in the
remnant basket. I've got some wonderful bar-
gains—cheap as dirt, but cleaner. (*Unwraps*

113

parcel). Look at these—a lovely pair of silk stockings, only two bob. (*Shows a pair of stockings without feet*). I know they've got no feet, but look how handy for muddy days. You just pull them right up your leg and they can't get splashed. (*Opens another parcel.*) Look at this lovely pair of gloves—one-and-eleven—this is the 'one' and that's the 'eleven.' Made of doe-skin—real dough, too—so if I don't use them as gloves I can make them into bread. Fancy these only one-and-eleven—of course, they are both for the right hand, so I shall only be able to wear one at a time, but that will be all right for they will last twice as long. Things were cheap. Do you know, they were selling penny postage stamps four for three-pence, and they'd only been used once. (*Unwraps another parcel.*) Now here's a bargain! A papier-mâché kettle—it can't boil over—if it gets too hot it just catches a light and puts the fire out. Things were cheap. Now I'll show you girls something that will make you sit up—it is some material I got for a new dress. (*Takes a piece of very loud material from out of parcel.*) Won't it look sweet when it's made up? If I don't like it as a dress I shall use it as a carpet. I think it's a cross between delphinium and trellis-work—I think I shall just have it hem-stitched to the knee and a puckered ruche on the selvedge edge and a wreath of minunots round the dado. (*She winds the material round herself to show the effect.*) I especially want to look coy for next Sunday to try and thaw Blue-beard's frozen heart. If he doesn't say he loves me when I've got this new dress on, then I shall give him notice. Do you know, I've been house-keeper to Bluebeard for thirty years come next Septuagesima Thursday and he hasn't pro-posed to me yet. There was only once when I thought he was going to pop the question—he came into my kitchen one morning when I was frying the sardines, and he said, 'Anne, I have a

burning pang within me—I have been lying
awake at night thinking of you and I have a
proposal to make.' I was just going to say 'This
is so sudden' when he finished his conversation
and said, 'Don't you ever give me Welsh Rarebit
again for supper—it always gives me nightmares'.
Oh, I was annoyed! I felt I should have
liked to have thrown the kitchen at him. But I
haven't lost hope yet—when this new dress is
made I'll vamp him. I'll wash my face with
Venus Soap and rub a bit of beetroot on my lips
like the other flappers do. Then if my name isn't
Mrs. Bluebeard within the week I'll either blow
out my brains or go on the stage.

(*Any song can be sung here or the following may be used.*)

SONG
(Air. 'I'll be Your Sweetheart')

When I put on my new dress next Sunday,
Then I'm sure I'll make our Bluebeard stare.
I hope he'll quickly name that *one* day
When I wear cherry-blossoms in my hair.
Then from that day I'll not be known as 'Miss'
When at the altar I shall murmur this:

REFRAIN
I'll be your Bluebird if you will be mine,
I'll get breakfast each morning at nine,
I'll cook your cutlets,
Steaks that you can chew,
Now you're a man—my plan
Will be to 'do' for you.

(Toby Trot *enters R.*)

TOBY: I'm Toby Trot—I'm very hot
And mad with indigestion,
And so Toby or not To-be,
That is, I think, the question.

115

Yes, and the answer's a lemon. And talking of lemons I've been sucking them all the time I was on the boat to prevent that mal-de-seasick. Everything in the water began to bubble so I sought the lemon-aid. I'm sorry I left London now, but it was too big to bring with me. I've come to these foreign parts with my sister Fatima—yes, Fatima is my sister.

> I've another sister, not so fat,
> She's like a concertina,
> She has all gone in,
> She's got so thin,
> We now all call her Lena.

I knew we should get shipwrecked before we started—you see, we brought a cargo of onions from Wales, so the ship was full of leeks. It was my sister Fatima who wanted to do this trip, so I came with her as a mascot.

> We both left home to cross the foam
> In spite of neighbours' scoff.
> But when both we, went off to sea,
> They came to see us off.

(Looking off-stage.) Why, whatever is this coming along?—It looks like a bundle of rhubarb tied up ugly,

(Re-enter Anne *L.)*

> Ah! maiden fair, don't be afraid
> I'm smitten with your charm,
> I'll promise you whate'er may come
> I'll guard you from all harm.

ANNE: That's very nice of you, but tell me, why do you speak so aerated? Are you the man who writes verses on Christmas cards?

TOBY: No—I'm just plain Toby Trot.

ANNE: Yes, you're plain enough.

116

TOBY: Well, you're no oil-painting, although your face is a bit greasy.

> That face of yours is what they call
> A Grecian, I suppose,
> Yes—it must be Grecian
> For you have a shiny nose.

ANNE: Now, stop that nonsense. Why do you always speak in rhyme?

TOBY: Well, I used to live in Limerick.

ANNE: And if you're not careful you'll die in Dartmoor. Well, now that we know each other so well, who are you—and why?

TOBY: I've just come here with my sister Fatima.

ANNE: Well, you mustn't mess about here—this is Bluebeard's Palace.

TOBY: Who's he?

ANNE: Do you mean to say you've never heard of Bluebeard?

TOBY: No. Is he Oxford or Cambridge?

ANNE: Neither. He belongs to an Eastern race, not a boat race.

TOBY: How was it he came to catch blue whiskers?

ANNE: Well, he was born with blue blood in his veins and he leaked.

TOBY: He must be like my fountain pen.

ANNE: It all came about once when he caught a cold and—

TOBY: I see—they didn't blow his nose, they *blew* his whiskers. What's his hobby anyhow?

ANNE: (*Whispering*) Wives! He collects them.

TOBY: Isn't it about time he collected you?

117

ANNE:	He'll want to marry me all right as soon as I have had my face lifted.
TOBY:	I shouldn't have it lifted, I should have it dropped—and stamped on. So this chap Bluebeards is a bit of a flirt.
ANNE:	Flirt! He's worse than that, he's a blue-blooded Mormon. As soon as he settles on one wife then off he goes and settles on another.
TOBY:	He's not a Blue*beard*—he's a blue *bottle*.
ANNE:	Well, he's a bit 'fly' anyhow. When he's about you take my advice and look after your sister Fatima.
TOBY:	If he is so fond of marrying it won't be Fatima he wants, he will prefer my other sister.
ANNE:	Why?
TOBY:	We call her Big Amy. Bigamy—see?
ANNE:	I'll give you such a smack in a minute.
TOBY:	If Bluebeard starts his little games I'll say, 'Now look here, Mister, This pretty Miss is my own sis And I'm here to assister'.
ANNE:	I do wish you'd stop talking like mottoes.
TOBY:	It's just a way I have they say No matter what mood *I'm* in, I don't rehearse but speak in verse I simply can't help rhyming.
ANNE:	Can you rhyme any word?
TOBY:	Of course I can.
ANNE:	Wait a minute, let me think. Rhyme 'appendicitis'.
TOBY:	(*Mumbling to himself as though thinking out a rhyme.*)

118

Some years ago a foreign foe
Came over here to fight us,
They'd no swords then, so used a pen,
And they died of appendicitis.

ANNE: Rotten!

TOBY: Well, you do better.

ANNE: Now Toby Trot your rhyming rot
Does give me such a headache,
And I am sure without a doubt
He is a lunatic.

TOBY: That doesn't rhyme.

ANNE: No, but it's true. But I say, do you think you could write a little verse in my autograph book? Something about my face.

TOBY: Yes I *could*, but if the police saw what I wrote I should get six months.

ANNE: But I should really like a pretty little verse that the canary could set to music.

TOBY: I know the idea—they call them sonnets. How would this do—

If I'd a face the same as yours,
And no young man would pat it,
I'd hang it on the garden fence
And throw some soft clay at it.

ANNE: Now there's no need to get personal. If I'm not handsome, I'm clever—I got a lot of marks when I was at school.

TOBY: So did I—I was always getting marks, but I won't say where. Anyhow, I was top of the class for truant playing.

ANNE: I was very good at school. I could do sums in my head.

TOBY: I could do them in my head all right, but I couldn't get them out.

ANNE: I'll see if you are any good at arithmetic.

DUET.

(*Air*—'*Three Blind Mice*')

ANNE: Three times twice. Three times twice
Three times twice then add on three,
I know what the answer's going to be.

TOBY: If you know the answer why ask me?

BOTH: Three times twice.

ANNE: One plus four. One plus four.
You cannot tell me I declare,
What is one plus four—so there.

TOBY: They are the trousers golfers wear.

BOTH: One plus four.

ANNE: Two and six. Two and six.
There's no need to stand there and frown,
Now what is two and six you clown.

TOBY: Why two and six is half-a-crown.

BOTH: Two and six.

ANNE: One from two. One from two.
Suppose I gave two eggs to you, Took one
away, now answer do.

TOBY: The answer is I'd still have two. (*Taking egg
from pocket.*)

BOTH: It's true. Too true.

ANNE: Two and one. Two and one.
This problem nearly always grips,
A man into a shop he nips.

TOBY: A tuppney dab and a pennorth of chips,

BOTH: Two and one.

ANNE:	One from nought. One from nought. If in my pocket cash I've none, To get a drink you think I'm done
TOBY:	I meet a friend who buys me one,
BOTH:	One from nought.
TOBY:	Two from one.
ANNE:	Can't be done.
TOBY:	Yes it can—now just obey, Lend me two shillings right away. (*Anne hands him coin.*) Now in my pocket that will stay (That's) *Two* from *one*.

(*Short dance. Exeunt L.*)

(*Enter* Bluebeard *R.*)

BLUEBEARD:	Behold I'm bumptious Bluebeard—the man of many wives, But should they disobey me then I take away their lives. I am a villain *doubled-dyed* of that you are aware. And that is why my beard's a different colour from my hair. All lovely women worship me and are anxious to get wed, And very oft their love for me will make them lose their head. So when I die and leave this Earth and then reincarnate, I'll perhaps come back to Earth again as Henry the Eighth. I oft decapitate my wives; it's quite a simple job. It does not take a moment now their hair has had a 'bob.' I quickly polish off the wives I'm anxious to expel. I am such a man of polish they have christened me 'Blue-*bell.*'

121

When e'er my wives gaze at this sword they tell
me it is vile.
I tell them it is my 'Gillette'—that's sure to '*ra-
zor*' smile.
I hang their heads up by their hair when they
have met their doom.
I have quite a dozen heads or more locked
up in yonder room.
And now another wife I seek to honour and
obey,
And if she disobeys my word then her I'll have
to slay.
My courtiers have told me that a maiden fair of
face,
Has landed on my Island here, but her I cannot
trace.

(*Takes large jewelled ring from off finger.*)

Oh ruby rare! My mystic gem! just grant me
one wish more,
Oh let me see this winsome maid who came
from distant shore.
They tell me that her lovely face is ever fair to
see,
Oh come and soothe my aching heart.

(Anne *rushes on R.*)

ANNE: (*Singing.*)   'I hear you calling me.'
(*She trembles as she sees* Bluebeard.)
Oh sire I your pardon beg—don't think me im-
polite,
Although I know it should be time I knew your
voice by sight.

(*She drops on her kness.*)

BLUEBEARD: Rise, you menial Jezebel! Go, find without
delay
The fair and comely maiden that I hear has
come this way.

122

ANNE: Pray put your noble mind at rest for there can
be no doubt,
The winsome maiden that you seek is waiting
now without.

BLUEBEARD: Then send her quickly to my side—this charmer
whom I seek,
And then within her shell-like ear sweet words
of love I'll speak.

ANNE: I'll hasten sire with utmost speed upon my little
trip,
I'll run at once with all my feet—so Toodle-oo
—Pip-pip!

(Exit R.)

(Song Bluebeard.*)*

*(Any suitable song can be introduced here, or the following
can be used.)*

(Air: 'The Bandolero.')

I'm not the chap called 'Nero,'
I'm not a seaside Pierrot,
I'm Bluebeard—a warm 'un,
A Mormon am I.
I chase the flappers, and if they refuse me,
Then I just chop off their 'nappers,'
It's Blackbird, good-bye.

(Anne re-enters R. followed by Toby and Fatima.
They all salaam.)

ANNE: Toby Trot and sister Fatima.

BLUEBEARD: Ye gods! what a dream of delight.

TOBY: *(To* Fat.*)* Hear what he called you—Turkish
Delight!

ANNE: Shush!

BLUEBEARD: *(To* Fat.*)* Come, fair maiden, you may kiss
my hand,
But stay, before you stoop,
I'll send away my servant Anne,

123

Also *(indicating* Toby*)* that nincompoop.

ANNE: *(To* Toby.*)* Hear what he called you?

TOBY: *(To* Blue.*)* You call me sir, a nincompoop,
And still my heart throbs on,
And I reply 'The same to you
With large thingumebobs on.'

(Exeunt Anne *and* Toby *R.)*

BLUEBEARD: And now, fair maid, we are alone,
First tell me who you are?

FATIMA: I'm a stranger to this island, I come from lands
afar.

BLUEBEARD: I do not care from whence you came, sweet
creature of my choice,
There is love within your star-like eyes and
music in your voice,
Your face is like an angel fair that dwelleth up
above,
So let me linger by your side while you just sing
of love.

(Fatima *can sing any love ballad here. After song* Bluebard
advances towards her.)

BLUEBEARD: Your voice has thrilled my inmost soul,
But now I must away
To make all preparations for our happy
wedding day. *(Exit L.)*

(Re-enter Toby *R.)*

FATIMA: Ah, Toby, there you are—what do you think?

TOBY: Eh?

FATIMA: I said 'What do you think?'

TOBY: I thought you said 'What do you *drink.*' Well,
go on I'll give it up.

FATIMA: That horrible man Bluebeard wants me to be
his wife.

124

TOBY: You can't marry a man with blue whis-
           kers—you may as well marry a Peacock.

FATIMA: But he told me it was a case of love at first sight.

TOBY: Tell him to have another look (*suddenly burst-
           ing into song to air of 'When we are Married.'*)
           When you are married what will you do?
           His teeth are white but his whiskers are *blue*,
           White teeth and blue whiskers will cause quite a
             stir
           You might as well marry a Seidlitz Pow*der*.

FATIMA·   Oh, Toby, how can you? If only that gallant
           Captain of our ship were here now—he would
           save me from my awful fate. Oh, I wish I were
           a man.

TOBY: So do I. I suppose you couldn't get married
           with a dog's licence—then you could bite old
           Bluebeard and he'd die of distemper.

FATIMA: Oh, what's to be done?

           (*Enter* Anne R.)

ANNE: Why, what's amiss?

TOBY: A Flapper.

ANNE: What *do* you mean?

TOBY: You said, 'What's a Miss?'—well a 'Miss' is a
           Flapper isn't it?

ANNE   (*To* Fatima.) What troubles you, dear?

FATIMA: Bluebeard has vowed he loves me and declares
           he will make me his wife.

TOBY: She mustn't marry Bluebeard—I should hate to
           have a brother-in-law who is a '*Blue-ter*'—I'd
           rather have a Red Herring.

ANNE: I've got an idea.

TOBY   Hold it tight.

FATIMA: If you can but help me you will earn my
            lifelong gratitude.

ANNE: I want to marry old Bluebeard myself. Give me
            your veil.

(Fatima *removes long veil she is wearing.* Anne *places it on her
                            head.*)

TOBY: (*To* Anne.) You look like a wedding cake that
            hasn't been whitewashed.

FATIMA: (*To* Anne.) How can I ever repay you?

TOBY: That's all right Sis. give *me* the fourpence and
            say no more about it.

ANNE: (*Dancing round stage with joy.*) I feel so gay in
            a bridal veil—I can smell the orange blossoms.

TOBY: No, that's my hair oil you can smell. Now be
            sure and don't let Bluebeard see your face, or
            he might re-christen you '*Anno*-Domini.'

                        TRIO

            (Fatima, Toby *and* Anne.)

            (*Air: 'He's a Jolly Good Fellow.'*)

ANNE: I'm going to marry old Bluebeard,
            (*To* Fat.) Though he is the fellow that *you*
            feared.

TOBY: I hope you will buy him a new beard.
            It's so conspicuous.

T. & F.   He is no good to us.

ANNE: You're only envious.

TOBY: But he looks a wicked old 'feller,'
            He wants a smack on the smeller.
            He cuts up his wives in the cellar.

ALL: But he won't murder us.

FATIMA: (*Looking off L.*) Hush! Here he comes—we must
            away.

126

TOBY:	Yes—let's 'congeal' ourselves, I think I'd better hide my head Or he may want to chop it, So Sister dear let us 'Avaunt;' In other words 'We'll hop it.' *(Exeunt* Fat. *and* Toby.*)*

(Anne remains standing with drooped head as Bluebeard enters.)

BLUEBEARD:	Ah pretty one, again we meet—your beauty makes me dizzy, Come, what's your name?
ANNE:	It's Clementine—but Mother calls me 'Lizzy.'
BLUEBEARD:	*(Hands her ring.)* Now take this ring. <div align="right">(Anne *does so.*)</div>We now are wed—that is my Country's custom, And now go fetch your bridal robes.
ANNE:	I'll just go home and dust'em.
BLUEBEARD:	To my Palace I will now away to make all preparation, The splendour of our wedding feast will cause a great sensation. I'll soon return and then, Sweetheart, we'll have a fond embrace. I'll lift that veil and place a kiss upon that lovely face. *(Exit* Bluebeard. *L.)*
ANNE:	I hope he won't be disappointed. He's a very touchy man—if he doesn't like faces he cuts them off and puts them in pickle. I'm rather sorry I've done this now.

(Enter Fatima.*)*

FATIMA:	Is all well?

127

ANNE: Yes, I think all is well, but I'm not.

FATIMA: Why—what do you mean?

ANNE: He gave me the ring, but I think you'd better have it after all. You look much nicer in this veil than I do. (*Puts veil on* Fatima's *head*.) Oh, you *do* look sweet—after all I think I should look nicer if my face were covered with a tarpaulin.

(*Exit R.*)

FATIMA: (*Calling after her.*) But—She's gone!

(*Re-Enter* Bluebeard.)

BLUEBEARD: Ah wife of mine I hand to you my bunch of precious keys,
All rooms within my Palace you can enter now with these.
But let me warn you not to use this large and rusty key.
For that one fits my private room where no ones goes but me.
And so dear wife don't dare to go into that secret room.
My other wives who've entered there have straightway met their doom.
So take that as a warning now before it is too late,
Or as sure as my name's Bluebeard you will meet a shocking fate.

(*Exit L.*)

FATIMA: I wonder what is within that secret room. Oh how he has excited my curiosity. Fancy giving a woman a key to a room and then telling her she must not enter there. Why it's as bad as buying a new hat and being told you must not put it on. (*Advancing towards L.*) I've a good mind to—

(Toby *Enters R.*)

TOBY: Fatima! the Captain is here.

FATIMA: Is he ashore?

128

TOBY: No—he's a Captain. He is just putting his ship ship-shape, and when he has got it the right shape he's coming here. You know Sis, I think he's in love with you.

FATIMA: What! the Captain?

TOBY: Yes. Now, I should like him for a brother-in-law.

FATIMA: Why?

TOBY: Well, he's so fond of the water, he might come home and help me clean out the cistern.

FATIMA: I'll hide myself until he comes, within that dark room yonder.
For absence, as the poets say, will make the heart grow fonder. (*Exit R.*)

TOBY: The lovers' toast I like the best,
Is one that's hard to beat:
'Here's to our Sweethearts and our Wives,
Let's hope they'll never meet.' (*Exit R.*)

(*Lively music of the hornpipe order. Enter the* Captain.)

SONG

Air. 'Good Ship Yacki-Hicki-Doo-La'

CAPTAIN: I'm the jolly Captain. Ha! ha! ha! ha!
From the good ship Caroline. He! he! he! he!
I've come here where the girls are prime,
For every jolly sailor likes his *mari-time.*
For there's a sweet girl here, her name's Fatima
No other girl is finer,
And I shall not stir till I've wed her,
On aboard of my ship Carolin*a.*
I am always on my mettle so they call me Captain Kettle,
For there never was a bigger *pot* than me.
And I cause a commotion for when I'm on the ocean,
There is bound to be a *swell* upon the sea.

129

In my uniform so grand they list to my command,
For I always keep my crew upon the fidge,
When dealing with the guards I know how to play my cards,
But I never have a *nap* when on the *bridge*.
In the summer Eighty-nine when first I crossed the line,
The sea was round so then we made a pause—
But still we thought we'd chance it, so we called the ship '*Sic* transit,'
For everybody on that vessel *was*.
But there, you don't want to hear about what I've done, it's what I'm going to do that matters. I've come in search of the fair Fatima. I must marry her and change her name, for Fatima sounds so greasy. (Fatima *to call off stage. She rushes on as though in fear.*) Why, what's the matter, you're shaking like a fly—have you seen a spider?

FATIMA: Worse than that. I went into yonder room and there were a dozen human heads hanging by their hair.

CAPTAIN: Why, it must be the Chamber of Horrors—it's sixpence extra to go in there. Did you see Madame Tussaud?

FATIMA: They were human heads that once had lived— human heads!

CAPTAIN: Well, I didn't think they were heads of celery. Where did you see all this?

FATIMA: But don't you understand? Bluebeard thinks I am his wife.

CAPTAIN: Does he? Well the quicker he *un*thinks the better. But what has really happened?

FATIMA: Well, Bluebeard thinks I am his wife, but his housekeeper put on this veil and took my place. But Bluebeard gave me the keys and told me I must not enter that room. He told

130

me tales of his other wives who had lost their heads.

CAPTAIN: You need never tell the old bounder—he will never know.

FATIMA: Yes, he will. Look, I dropped the keys upon the floor, and look, now this one is stained with dye.

CAPTAIN: Oh, so the keys die, too. Don't worry, my ship is waiting on the *quay* we'll give him that one. But stay, there is another key I wish to give you.

FATIMA: Indeed. What key is that?

CAPTAIN: The *key* to my heart, because you I *a-door.* When shall our wedding be!

FATIMA: But we may not be spared to have a wedding—Bluebeard may kill us both.

CAPTAIN: In that case—when shall our funeral be? Name the day and tell me, will you have lilies or lilac?

FATIMA: This is no time for jest.

CAPTAIN: Perhaps you think I can't be serious, but I can. Surely you don't doubt the sincerity of a British sailor. (*Embraces her.*)

FATIMA: No, but—

CAPTAIN: Ah, you don't care for me.

FATIMA: I do.

CAPTAIN: Is that the truth? Then tell me so in song.

(*Any love duet can be introduced here or the following may be used to the air of 'The Reign of the Roses.'*)

DUET

FATIMA: Love, I do not doubt you.

131

| CAPTAIN: | I can't live without you. |
| | Makes my heart pine. |

| FATIMA: | Say will you be true dear. |

| CAPTAIN: | Yes true dear for ever, |
| | My love naught can sever. |

| BOTH: | When you dear are mine. |

(*They walk towards exit R. when the gruff voice of* Bluebeard *is heard.*)

FATIMA: (*Alarmed.*) Hark, 'tis he. Hide, and if I require help I will call you.

CAPTAIN: Don't worry dear, a Captain is always on the watch. If Bluebeard starts any of his little games, I'll hoist the Blue Peter and come to *see.* Don't be afraid little one. (*He kisses her and runs off L.* Bluebeard *Enters R.*)

BLUEBEARD: Now winsome wife hand me the key—the large one that is rusted,
What's this? A stain upon the key! So *you* cannot be trusted.
You've entered in my secret room as I anticipated,
And so like my other wives you'll be decapitated.

(*Takes sword from out belt.*)

I'm grieved to spoil your pretty neck, I've never seen one whiter,
(*He forces* Fatima *on her knees.*)

Prepare now for the fatal blow, (*Raises sword.*)

(*Captain rushes on and grabs* Bluebeard *by his uplifted arm.*)

CAPTAIN: Stop that you fat old blighter!

(*Captain takes* Fatima *in his arms.* Bluebeard *drops sword and looks on amazed.*)

BLUEBEARD: Pray who are you that you should come and thwart me in my plans?

CAPTAIN: I'm showing you how gentlemen behave in other lands.

BLUEBEARD: Be carefull, or I'll call my guard and lead you to your slaughter.

CAPTAIN: I don't want to see your guard. I'd rather have a porter.

BLUEBEARD: That woman wears my wedding ring, so you've no need to linger.

(*Enter* Anne *L.*)

ANNE: You'll pardon me but in mistake you placed it on *my* finger.

BLUEBEARD: What! *you* my wife?

ANNE: Of course I am,
You see we're rightly wedded.

BLUEBEARD: If that's the case I'll go at once and get *myself* beheaded.

ANNE: You won't wed me?

BLUEBEARD: Indeed I won't—I haven't pluck to do so.

ANNE: All right I'll marry Toby now—I cannot waste my trousseau.

(Toby *enters L.* Anne *rushes and embraces him.*)

Toby can I be your wife—I hope you've no objection.

TOBY: As I'm collecting curios you can go in my collection.

(Fatima *and* Captain *come forward.*)

FATIMA: In you my dear I've drawn a prize—a husband who's a frank one.

133

CAPTAIN: So Bluebeard is the odd man out—He's only
               drawn a blank one.

FATIMA: (*To* Bluebeard.) In fact you are a wicked man;
               your methods have been awful,
               Why not reform and promise us you'll lead a
               life that's lawful.

               (Bluebeard *holds jewel in his right hand.*)

BLUEBEARD: I swear my future will be good—my life shall be
               untainted.

ALL: Hurray!

BLUEBEARD: We'll dine within my Palace grand—you're one
               and all invited,
               Will you gather round my festive board?

ALL: We all shall be delighted.

BLUEBEARD: I'll no more lead the life I've led with murders
               intermingled,
               I'll cast away this cursed beard.
                                        (*Throws beard off.*)

ANNE: Oh, look old Bluebeard's shingled!

FINAL CHORUS

(*Any bright up-to-date tune can be used, or the following
words can be sung to the air of 'Men of Harlech.'*)

ALL: Now the tale of Bluebeard's ended,
               Everything has turned out splendid,
               Love and friendship now are blended.
               Joy now reigns supreme.

FATIMA: Of love I have full measure.

CAPTAIN: I have won a real treasure.

TOBY: Tho' my bride may be shop-soiled,

134

ANNE: You can have me renovated at your leisure.

BLUEBEARD: Now to show I bear no malice,
             We will go into my Palace,
             Drink rich wines from out the chalice.

ALL: Hip! Pip! Pip! Hurray!

BABES IN THE WOOD

(1931)

CHARACTERS:
Baron Oofless
Reggie ⎫
Cissie ⎭ The Babes
Marion (The Baron's daughter)
Nick ⎫
Dick ⎭ The Robbers

SCENE: The Wood. Curtains. A row of shrubs along back. A dilapidated sign-post marked 'To Sleepy Wood.' Rustic fence to convey entrance to wood. Log of tree up back to be used as seat. Anything to suggest exterior appearance can be added to scene.

OPENING MUSIC might be 'Down in the Forest.' If possible, the words to be sung off stage by choir.

ENTER THE BARON

(He is a man something after the John Bull type.)

BARON: My name is Baron Oofless—a most unpleasant gent,
My pockets too are *barren* for I haven't got a cent.
I'm so *hard* up I'm *stoney,* and I tell you that's no joke,
For I cannot go on pleasure *bent* because I'm always *broke.*
I've heard it said that money talks; well, that I won't deny,
But the only time it speaks to me is when it says 'Goodbye.'
If I can't get some money soon I'm sure I shall go daft,
I wish that I could raise the *wind* and get an over*draft.*
Although I'm owner of a farm my crops seem so unkind,
No matter what the seeds I sow they always change their mind,

137

For every time I plant my wheat it dies and disappears,
I think it hears the cawing crows—they say that wheat has
  ears.
No matter how I till the soil just nothing ever grows;
The only corn I ever get are corns upon my toes.
Now if I put potatoes in they never even rise;
And if they do they all wear *specs* or have tears in their
  eyes.
If something doesn't happen soon to alter my position,
I shall have to break into a bank or file a *partition*.
The only cash my family had was held by my late brother,
But in his will he left me out and willed it to another.
He left his fortune to his Babes and they alone can clutch it,
And so until those youngsters die I'm not allowed to touch
  it.
If I could only find a way to polish off those kidlets,
Then I should be much better off with bags and bags of
  quidlets.
Those wretched brats are in my care—the darlings, how I
  hate 'em!
If I could only find a way to gently spiflicate 'em,
For once those babes are cleared away then I shall have
  their riches.
Now every time I think of them my palm gets hot and it-
  ches.

SONG

(Air—'The Bogie Man.')

When my brother 'kicked the bucket,' much to everybody's
  grief,
He left his babies in my care, I said 'That's O K Chief.'
A tear I shed, then hung my head, to hide my evil grin,
Ah! curse them! How I hate those brats! I'm going to 'do them
  in.'

> Hush, hush, hush, I want to find a plan,
> To get rid of my brother's kids as quickly as I can.
> Tush, tush, tush, though I'm their guardian,
> I'm going to do for both the two
> As quickly as I can.

The question now that worries me is how to do the deed,
When putting babes 'upon the spot' the best way to proceed,
When settling children's hash, methinks, one mustn't make a
   hash.
I'll get a 'crook' their 'goose to cook' and help me get the cash.

Hush, hush, hush, I think I've found a plan,
To get rid of my brother's kids as quickly as I can,
Shush, shush, shush, I'll go and hire a man
To do the job for couple of bob,
Like Edgar Wallace can.

*(Short dance and exit R. He re-enters at once, Dick enters L.
He is a horrible-looking ruffian. Large black slouch hat,
sword sticking in belt, etc.)*

BARON *(seeing* Dick): Ah! a stranger in the wood.
                              With happiness I greet you.
Though I've seen things like you in cheese, I'm very pleased
   to meet you.
But who *are* you?

DICK: Why, don't you know?

BARON: No, I'm no good at riddles.

DICK *(looking coy)*: Why, I'm the fairy of this glade.

BARON: Now stop those taradiddles.

DICK: Well, if the truth you wish to learn, I'm just a fearsome
   robber,
I am one who greatly needs re-*dress,* you can see that by my
   clobber.
And here within this mystic wood with sparrows I'm hob-
   nobbin',
For I'm one of two jail birds.

BARON: Your breed must be the *robbin'.*

DICK: My name is Dick.

BARON: What, *Dirty* Dick? For you look quite untidy.

DICK: The reason why I look so is my bath night's not till
   Friday.

I have a partner, Nick by name, who also lives on crime,
And when he doesn't *steal* away he just sits *killing* time.
The crimes and murders we have done would really make a
nice list.

BARON: Then perhaps you'll do a job for me?

DICK: *(handing pamphlet)*: With pleasure. Take a price list.

BARON: I'm much obliged. Now give me, please, your very
best quotation.
But before we start on business let us stop this recitation.

DICK: Tho' Panto pro's don't speak in prose, I see no rhyme
or reason.
Why we can't hie from 'neath this tree—they can't call that
high treason.
(Changing his tone) I am very pleased you suggested changing that rhyming talk.

BARON: Well, I thought it was getting a bit monotonous.

DICK: It wasn't so much that, but I've been wanting to tell you
for a long time about my partnership.

BARON: Well, why didn't you?

DICK: Because I couldn't rhyme 'partnership.'

BARON *(looking at list)*: I see you call yourselves *Messrs.* Nick
and Dick. I can quite understand you both being *Messers.*
Which are you?

DICK: I told you—I'm Dick.

BARON: Dick what?

DICK: Just plain Dick.

BARON: Yes, you're *plain* enough. A few more pimples and
they'd call you spotted Dick. Where *did* you get that face
from?

DICK: It was a present from my mother.

BARON: Had she a grudge against you?

DICK: She gave me this face on the day I was born.

BARON: I see; a sort of birthday mug *(indicating mouth)*—pity about that crack in the middle of it. But tell me, Dick, isn't your name really Richard?

DICK: Yes, but Dick is my *nick* name.

BARON: You can't have a *nick* name—you are Dick. Your partner's Nick.

DICK: They only christened him Nick because he wasn't well at the time.

BARON: What had that got to do with it?

DICK: Well, you see, Nick wasn't up to Dick. He was called Nick ever since he was a baby, and he has been on the *nick* ever since. He always had such *taking* ways. I didn't have the nick-knacks, so they called me Dick. Mother couldn't tell which was which.

BARON: How did she know which was Nick and which was Dick?

DICK: Well, Nick wore knickers and Dick wore a Dicky. But we were two such lovely babes.

BARON: Ah! Babes! That is what I want to talk to you about.

DICK *(indicating tree stump)*: Come in the office. Let us sit on the *wood* and have a *board* meeting.

(They sit.)

BARON: I have two babes under my care for which I don't care. And as long as they live I have to remain a poor man.

DICK: Oh, my poor man!

BARON: But should they die then I become rich. But how can they die?

DICK *(holding up warning finger)*: Shush! Don't talk too loud. Remember, earwigs have ears.

BARON: Yes, but don't tell me they wear wigs too.

DICK: I think I can arrange that little request for you. Have a look at the price list I gave you. It will give all the information you want. I will go and fetch my partner. He has just gone into the woods to shoot some holes in frogs, as we are having toad-in-the-hole for supper.

(Exit Dick, *L.)*

BARON: *(reading price list)*: 'Messrs. Nick and Dick: Murderers. Crimes of all description carried out by skilled workmen. Families waited on daily. Our motto is "Cleanliness and Civility." Small murders from three and sixpence, cash with order. Poison from four and six per gallon delivered daily in our own plain vans. Highway robberies carried out with swiftness and despatch. Houses burnt down while you wait.' *(Away from book.)* The very firm I've been looking for. I'd better fill in the order form and post it off at once.

(Dick enters L. followed by Nick.)

DICK: *(to Baron)*: Here is the whole of the firm. My partner, Mr. Nick.

BARON: Hullo, *Old Nick.* Glad to know you.

NICK: I'm sorry to hear that. What is this little job you want jobbed?

BARON: Just a couple of children I want to get rid of.

NICK: Children? They're easy—we just squash them under our feet like this—*(illustrates)*—same as you would a cockroach.

BARON: I want you to kill the kids while they are sleeping.

NICK: I see. So that they wake up dead. How big are the kids?

BARON: With their socks on they are about so high *(indicates)*.

NICK: You mean, they stand just above *two feet.*

BARON: Yes, excepting when they stand on their heads.

DICK: As our sale is now on, we'll do the job a bit cheaper.

NICK: Our usual price is four shillings a yard. Let me see—two feet, that's a yard and a half. Suppose we say seven and six for the two.

142

BARON: Where did you learn your mental arithmetic—in a mental home? Seven and six is a bit more than I wanted to pay.

NICK: That's really very cheap. You couldn't get it done cheaper at Woolworths.

DICK: You want them *thoroughly* killed, don't you?

BARON: How much would you charge for just tying a brick round their necks and chucking them in a pond?

NICK: That would be more. You see, the brick would cost us tuppence.

DICK: You leave it to us, Gov'nor—we'll do it all right. You might fill in the order form. We have to keep our accounts in order for the Income Tax inspector. (Baron *signs book.* Dick *calls to* Nick.) Nick, forward—sign!

(Nick *comes forward and signs as they would in a draper's shop.*)

NICK *(to* Baron*)*: How about a bit on account?

BARON: I never pay in advance.

DICK: But suppose after we've done 'em in you refuse to pay us?

BARON: Then you have the babes.

DICK: But what should we be able to do with a couple of dead kids?

BARON: You could hang them on your watch chain as mascots.

NICK: All right—we'll do it. But don't forget to recommend us to your friends.

BARON: Certainly. Give me a few of your cards. I'll send them to all my relations at Christmas time. By the way, I have a man living next door to me who is learning the cornet. He will be the next one I shall want popped off.

DICK: Right. Cornet players are our speciality. We *blow* them out.

NICK: Let's fix things up. We'll call at your house and collect the kids—we'll kid the kids we're going to take them to the pictures. Then we'll bring 'em here and *(runs finger across his throat and making noise with mouth)*—and they'll never know what it is to have the toothache again.

DICK: It's understood we kill the babes and quickly stop their squealing,
And now we'll have a song and dance to show there's no ill feeling.

TRIO (Baron, Dick *and* Nick.)

(Air' Three Blind Mice.')

ALL: We're three bad men. Three bad men.

BARON: We're murderous villains and fond of strife.

NICK: Think nothing of taking a guinea-pig's life.

DICK: As we cut off his tail with a carving knife.

ALL: Three bad men.
    We're three bad men. Three bad men.
    There's nothing that's wicked we will not do,
    From pulling cat's tails to make them mew,
    To giving a spider a fly to chew,
    Three bad men.

    We're three bad men. Three bad men.
    We lie in wait upon little boys,
    And threaten them quick if they make a noise,
    Then grab all their sweets and collar their toys,
    Three bad men.

    We're three bad men. Three bad men.
    We hang behind trams and we never pay,
    At night when it's dark and we're out to play,
    We pull front door bells and then run away.
    Three bad men.

    We're three bad men. Three bad men.
    We know very well we'll end in jail,
    For tying tin cans on the old dog's tail,
    And drowning tiddlers in mother's pail,
    Three bad men.

(Short dance and exit, L.)

(Enter Marion, *R.).*

(She is dressed as a simple country girl.)

MARION: I have a strange presentiment, for something seems
to say
A wicked plot is brewing to take the Babes away.
For last night in my dreams I saw my cousins hand in hand
With two big burly ruffians—why, I couldn't understand.
And now,when walking through the wood, I saw two ruffians
there
Conversing with my father with a most mysterious air.
I know my father hates the twins, though I cannot reason
why,
For once I heard him murmur: 'How I wish those brats
would die!'
So I am here to do my best if danger should arise,
And I've a token of good luck—a token that I prize.
'Tis just a four-leaf shamrock a gipsy gave to me,
Who told me lots of tales of its wondrous history.
She told me when in case of need that all I had to do
Was just to kiss this shamrock twice to make my wish come
true.
So now I ask my mascot true to lend its magic charm
To safely guard those darling Babes and keep them from all
harm.   *(She walks towards Exit.)*
Before I go perhaps I'd better sing a little lay;
It will help to drown my sorrow and cheer me on my way.
Besides, I know within this wood good fairies often hide,
And perhaps the music of my song will bring them to my
side.
My lucky charm I'll give to them and make my one request.
And now I'll sing my fairy song and just hope for the best.

SONG

(Suggested song, 'There are Fairies at the Bottom of my Gar-
den,' or any song of this nature. If possible, a few little fairy
dancers might come on here and join Marion *in dance at*
the end of her song. If it is not possible to introduce the
dancers, Marion *might make her exit before the end of song,*
still singing—this to give the effect of her voice dying away
in the distance.)

145

(Enter Nick *R. He is leading* Reggie *by the hand.)*

*(*NOTE—*it is optional for the parts of the Babes to be played as comedy children or just as straight characters.)*

NICK: Now we're in the forest here I'll show you all the wonders.

That tree was struck by lightning; now it trembles when it thunders.

We've got some lovely acorns here that grow as big as bunions;

The dandelions are so strong they smell like Spanish onions.

REGGIE: I don't want to go with you—can't I go back to Nunky? *(Trembles.)*

NICK: Now stop that shaking—have no fear. My word, you do look funky.

REGGIE: I don't like you—do you like me?

NICK: Do I like you—yes, rather!

Why, every time I take a step I feel I'm your *step-father.*

REGGIE *(crying)*: I want to go back to my home.

NICK: Now stop those tears and *dry* up.

Or you'll get water on the brain if that moisture gets too high up.

REGGIE: Where has my sister Cissy gone?

NICK: I can't think how we've missed her *(looks off).*

My partner's got her by the hand, so your sister he'll assist her.

Now when they come we'll roam the woods, and if you both are willing.

We'll make you die of laughter and have a time that's killing.

So cheer up, son, and dry those tears and stop your woeful whining.

Let me give your face a polish up and start the *son* a-shining.

(Rubs Reggie's *face with handkerchief.* Cissy's *voice is heard off calling 'Reg! Reggie!')*

REGGIE: I hear my sister calling me.

NICK: She gave me quite a start, Reg.
    You're sure that is your sister's voice?—it sounds more like
    a partridge.

(Cissy enters, R.)

REGGIE: Come to my arms, my darling sis. Whatever made
    you *stay* there?

CISSIE *(tearfully)*: I thought I'd lost you in the wood.

(Reggie and Cissie embrace.)

NICK: Now, then, break *away* there.

(Dick enters, R.)

DICK *(to Nick)*: We'd better get on with the job; we've got no
    time for yapping.
    So now we're in the Sleepy Wood we'll start the kid
    kidnapping.

NICK: I think I'd like to have a rest—that's far more to my
    liking;
    Through walking all those weary miles my feet have started
    'iking (aching).

CISSIE: Let's play a game to cheer us up—these woods make
    me feel creepy.

DICK: Well, how about a game of *nap* as soon as you feel
    sleepy?

REGGIE: Kiss in the ring I'd like to play.

NICK: Well, take the hand of Cissy's
    And Dick and I will be the ring and you can be the kisses.

*(Nick and Dick take hold of hands and encircle Reggie and
Cissy. They dance round child-like, both singing in silly
high-pitched voices, 'Now you're married we wish you joy,
first a girl and then a saveloy.' They all get mixed up. Nick
and Dick kiss each other in mistake for the Babes. Babes
laugh. General comic business as they all fall down at the
finish.)*

*(*Nick *brings* Dick *down stage and speaks to him in a loud whisper.)*

NICK: What are we to do now, Dick? I think we'll run away.

DICK: We've got to kill the youngsters first, and that without delay.

NICK: What! Kill the kids! I feel I can't. I couldn't even strike 'em,
  For since we've got 'em in the woods I've quite begun to like 'em.

DICK: You'll have to stab them both, I say. You've got your sword for sticking.

NICK: But you don't, somehow, see my *point*. It's my conscience that is pricking.

DICK:*I* don't feel I can kill the kids, although we've both been paid to;
  I've suddenly come over good.

NICK: I believe you are afraid to.
  We've both been hired for this job, so surely it's worth doin',
  So if we now throw up the job we shall bring our firm to ruin.

REGGIE *(aside to* Cissy*)*: I'm sure they mean to do us harm. Oh, why did they select us?

CISSIE: Let's go and seek for Marion—I'm sure she will protect us.

*(*Reggie *and* Cissie *both tiptoe off, L.)*

DICK: You mean to say you'll chuck the job! Well, you're a pretty beauty.
  Remember, you won't get what's due if you neglect your duty.

NICK: *You* kill the kids.

DICK: I can't today, for I'm not feeling vicious.
  Besides, today is Friday and you know I'm superstitious.

NICK: Remember that the Baron said he couldn't tolerate them.

DICK: Well, let him do his dirty work; I just can't spiflicate them. *(Dick takes coin from his pocket.)*
Let's toss this coin. It's head you win. You call, and if you fail—— *(Tosses coin.)*

NICK: That penny hasn't got a head.

DICK: Ah, thereby hangs a tail.
We'll fight a duel who'll do the deed; the loser mustn't miss one. *(Hold out long and short sword.)*

Come on, choose your weapon now. One moment—I'll have this one. *(Takes long sword.)*

(They fight a comic duel. Stand in opposite corners of stage and advance towards each other with eccentric walk. Then they follow each other round stage, getting eventually into a run. One drops sword, the other picks it up and sharpens it on his own sword after style of butcher. He might use sword to sharpen his pencil with for the 'score.' Any comic business can be introduced here. At finish they both fall with the others' sword sticking from under their arms as though they have been stabbed. After lying on floor for a few seconds they both sit up.)

NICK: What! *you* alive?

DICK: What! *you* alive?

BOTH: Look where my dagger's sticking.

NICK: There's no doubt we are both alive.

DICK *(he kicks Nick)*: Both alive and kicking.

(They both get up from floor and look round.)

NICK: The kids have gone. They've run away.

DICK: I didn't somehow miss 'em.
They didn't even say 'good-bye.'

NICK: Or stop to let me kiss 'em.

149

DICK: It's funny where those kids have gone. My brain it starts to addle.

NICK: I suppose when we began to fight it made those kids skedaddle.

DICK *(looking off, L.)*: That must be the path they took when from us they departed.

NICK *(pointing R.)*: Well, we'd best go the other way and meet 'em 'fore they've started. *(Exeunt, R.)*

*(*Reggie *and* Cissy *enter, L.)*

REGGIE: Oh, sister dear, I think we're lost.

CISSY: But where are our two Nunkies?

REGGIE: They're no relation to us, Cis; they're just two artful monkeys.

CISSY: I wonder why they brought us here? They must have had a reason.
Our love they want to conquer, p'raps.

REGGIE: No; conkers aren't in season.
But never mind. I'll stick to you, for I'm your big, tall brother.

CISSY: Although I am *far-the-less*, I'll love you like a mother.

SONG

(Air—'Oh, Mr. Porter.')

CISSY: Oh, brother Reggie, what shall we do?
If we could find dear Marion she'd help both me and you.

REGGIE: Don't worry, sister; I will just do all I can
To outwit both those ruffians and upset their evil plan.

(A short dance could be introduced here.)

CISSY *(crying)*: Boo hoo! I am so hungry.

REGGIE: Now don't you start or you'll make me cry again.

CISSY: Men don't cry.

150

REGGIE: Yes, they do. I was coming through the village the other day when I saw a great big man with a bell in his hand and they told me he was the town crier.

CISSY: What did he cry for?

REGGIE: Because people *paid* him. He had to cry to get his food.

CISSY: Boo hoo! Well, that's I'm crying for.

REGGIE: We'll go into the woods and find some nice big blackberries and we'll have them for supper.

CISSY: Oh yes, we'll have a large mushroom for our table. But what can we sit upon.

REGGIE: We can sit upon the toad stools. And then we'll go down to the stream and get some lovely crystal water in a buttercup.

CISSY: But how shall we know when it's time go to bed?

REGGIE: I think we can keep a watch on the berries by the water.

CISSY: That won't tell us the time.

REGGIE: Yes, it will. That will be our *water-berry watch.*

CISSY: Don't you be so silly, Reggie. I know what we can do— we can blow one of those puff balls—they always tell the right time.

REGGIE: No; we'll go to bed at the same time as the birds have their custard for supper.

CISSY: They don't have custard.

REGGIE: Of course they do; they make it with Bird's Custard Powder.

(Here the stage lights are to be lowered.)

CISSY: Oh, it's getting dark. Let us go and sleep and forget all our troubles.

REGGIE: All right, Cissy dear, we will. *(Points off,* R.*)* Let us both lie down beneath that bower of roses, and perhaps we shall dream of Fairyland.

(A short lullaby to be played here. Or the following might be used. Air—'The Alabama Coon.')
Let us go and sleep beside the roses
　　Underneath the silv'ry shining moon.
Hush-a-by, don't you cry, the fairies will protect us,
　　And someone's sure to find us very soon.

(Exeunt, R., embracing.)

(Lights to be lowered. Here it will be necessary to convey the passing of time. This is to be done by Father Time *crossing stage slowly. He is wearing a long flowing cloak, long beard and long-haired wig. He carries an hour-glass and scythe. If another character is not possible, it will be found quite simple for* Nick *or* Dick *to double this part. After exit of* Father Time, *lights up.)*

Baron *enters, L.*

(He walks with a weary gait and looks about.)

BARON: Though many moons have been and gone since I was
　　at this spot,
I remember well that it was here I hatched that deadly plot
To haste the Babes' untimely end. Oh, why did I suggest it!
And now I'm filled with sad remorse and find I can't digest
　　it.
I must find some means to get them back—some method
　　that is surer.
I suupose, to find my brother's *heirs,* I want some hair
　　restorer.
If I could find those robbers, too, I would, with their
　　permission,
Ask them to save the precious Babes and pay them their
　　commission.
Ah! here they come, those villains bold—the sight it makes
　　me shudder.
I'm all at sea—just like a ship that's been and lost its
　　rudder.

152

(Enter Nick *and* Dick.*)*

So at last we meet. Where are the babes?

NICK: We don't know. We just mislaid them.

BARON: Then you didn't kill them?

DICK: No, Gov'nor. We just couldn't do it.

NICK: It was like this. We brought them here to this spot and Dick and I were just having a friendly fight between our two selves, when the two Babes just slipped away.

DICK: They just vanished like two ice creams in a frying pan.

BARON: So you didn't carry out your dirty deed?

NICK: Indeed, no.

BARON: Poor little things! Do you realise what you have done? You have left them to roam the forest alone and by now they must have lost their way.

DICK *(sobbing)*: Poor little things! Perhaps by now they may be resting on some nasty stinging nettle.

NICK *(sobbing)*: It is all your fault, Dick, you wicked man! By rights they should have been killed in comfort.

(Nick *and* Dick *go on their knees to the* Baron.)

NICK *and* DICK: Forgive us. Don't treat us too harshly.

BARON: Rise, my brave fellows. Don't cry; you are breaking my heart.
(Changing tone.) I will double your pay for what you haven't done. *(Hands them purse.)* For ever since that day when last we met I have learned to love those Babes.

NICK *and* DICK: Same here.

BARON: But how can you say you loved the Babes when you tell me you have lost them?

DICK: Because it is better to have loved and lost than not to have loved at all.

NICK: We must find them somehow, by hook or by crook.

DICK: Well, you're a crook, so take your hook.

NICK: I don't know how to catch babes—what bait do you use?

BARON: We must find the Babes at any cost,
For if they aren't found then *we* are lost.

TRIO

(Air—'After the Ball.')

After the Babes we'll wander,
And look for them high and low,
We've made up our minds to find them,
No matter where we've to go.
As soon as we find the darlings
Have answered to our call,
We'll all play a game and start running—
After the ball.

(Dance and Exeunt, R.)

(Enter Marion, L.)

MARION: Those precious Babes are missing still; whatever has
come o'er them?
The days have just seemed endless since the last time that I
saw them.
I'll journey to the wishing well along the path down yonder,
And hope that I might find the way to where those Babes
do wander.
I fear they've rambled in the wood with danger all around
them.
I vow I will not rest content until someone has found them.
I'll roam the forest through and through; I'll find them
come what may.
If wishing will not bring them to me then love will find a
way.

(? SONG. Exit Marion, L.)

*(Babes enter, R. They might now be wearing clothes which are
too short for them, to convey that they have grown up since
last seen. They look about themselves in surprise.)*

154

CISSY: Oh, Reggie dear, I know this place—it seems to make me creep.

REGGIE: Why, this is where we wandered from before we went to sleep.

CISSY: 'Twas here those ruffians had their fight—

REGGIE: And where we heard their plot.

CISSY: Oh, yes, it all comes back to me; I hate this horrid spot.

REGGIE: Oh, Cissy, look, your dress has shrunk—it doesn't look your own.

CISSY: I wonder why we look so strange.

REGGIE: I know, we both have grown.
　　We must have been asleep so long we've grown out of our clothes.
　　What all the birds must think of us—well, goodness only knows.
　　They may think you're a sparrow.

CISSY: And you perhaps a crow.
　　Well, let us do a little dance and then they soon will know.

(Dance.)

*(*Marion *enters. She rushes at* Babes *and embraces them.)*

MARION: The Babes! the Babes! My darling Babes, I've found you both at last.
　　Where have you been—what have you done? The time has slowly passed.

REGGIE: Those ruffians brought us to this wood, but away we softly crept.

CISSY: And then we found a mossy bank and from that time we slept.

MARION: And so my lucky shamrock now has made my wish come true,
　　And guided me along the path and brought me safe to you.

*(*Baron *enters.)*

155

BARON: What's this I see? My children dear. Ah! now I am contented.

REGGIE: But once you said you hated us.

BARON: Since then I have repented.

(Nick *and* Dick *enter. They are now clean and smartened up.)*

BARON: But who is this?

NICK: Why, don't you know?

BARON: I don't—pray tell me quick.

DICK: Why, I am Dick—of course I am.

NICK: And I'm his partner Nick.

BARON: It can't be true; of my old friends you don't bear any traces.
What have you done?

DICK: Oh, nothing much—we've only washed our faces.

NICK: And, what's more, we have both reformed and now we have no vices.

DICK: We're both as gentle as can be and make pets of white mices.

(*Nick takes Dick aside.)*

NICK: I don't think 'mices' sounds correct—you surely should be wiser.

DICK: Well, what *is* plural for 'mice'?

NICK: I think it must be 'miser'—
That's what they teach at public schools.

DICK: You mean at public houses.

NICK: I think when meaning lots of mice they always call them 'mouses.'

BARON: We don't want any secrets here, so come and join the party.

156

MARION: For now the Babes are safely back we're happy, hale and hearty.

BARON: As I am full of joy just now I hope you'll come and share it.
But promise first you will be good.

DICK: We will.

NICK: We will—we swear it.

MARION: As bad beginnings always seem to have their happy ends,
Let us one and all join hands, for now we're loyal friends.

NICK *and* DICK: We promise in the future we will always be so good.

REGGIE *and* CISSY: So this ends up the story of the Lost Babes in the Wood.

FINALE

(Air—'Il Bacio.')

So it ends now,
We are friends now
So give a kind cheer, just before you all go.
'Twill reward us
To applaud us,
To say you've been liking our show.
We've all done our best
And worked with a zest—
Just for your delight.
We say—we all hope you may
Come again some other night.
Now we wish you
A fond Adieu.
Just hoping we've all made ourselves understood!
Change your tears, then,
For loud cheers, then,
Give a cheer for the Babes in the Wood.

LITTLE BO-PEEP

(1933)

CHARACTERS:
Bo-Peep
Dame Trot
Nicadeem
Boy Blue
Baron
Fairy

SCENE: To represent a country glade. A large tree trunk rises from centre of stage to represent base of tree, this to stand a few feet away from backing so that entrances and exits may be made behind same. Moss or imitation grass should run along entire back. A few large evergreens, etc.
Choir to be singing off stage L. as curtain rises. Any madrigal could be introduced here, but the following should be sung in conclusion. The singing to gradually die away when Nicadeem enters.

Finale of Chorus

Now then Boy Blue come blow your horn
For little Bo-Peep is all forlorn.
If she doesn't find you, oh what will she do?
Her heart is just pining for Mister Boy Blue.

(Nicadeem *enters* R.)

(*He walks toward L. and shakes his fist at the voices off stage.*)

NICADEEM: Shut up that row—away with you,
I hate the very name 'Boy Blue';
The thought of him just makes me creep,
For he's the one who loves Bo-Peep.

(Comes down stage.)

I'm Nicadeem—a selfish elf—
I think of no one but myself,
I roam these woods by night and day
And capture all that come my way.
They tell me I've a heart of stone,
That may be true, but still I own
For one I have affection deep,
A pretty maiden named Bo-Peep.
If all my plans go right then she
Will very şoon belong to me.
I walk these woods in this disguise
In hope to catch her by surprise,
And then I'll take her in my arms
And gaze upon her lovely charms;
But if she cries aloud with fear,
I'll kill each one who ventures near,
They're filled with awe when me they see,
I scare them all.

(Fairy appears from behind tree trunk.)

FAIRY: Excepting me.

NICADEEM: Why, who are you—you saucy jade,
        Of imps like you I'm not afraid,
        To satisfy my fiendish whim
        I'd tear your carcase limb from limb.

FAIRY: Such spite on me none can bestow,
        For I'm immortal you must know,
        A fairy small from out the dell,
        I live within a sweet blue bell,
        About these woods I slowly creep
        To see no harm comes to Bo-Peep.

NICADEEM: But she will soon belong to me.

(Fairy shakes her head.)

She will I say.

FAIRY: Ah well—we'll see.

(Fairy *disappears behind tree stump.*)

(Nicadeem *rushes off R.*)

(Dame *enters L.*)

DAME: Oh no, my dears. *I'm* not Bo-Peep, although
I'm young and skittish,
I'm just a simple English girl, my motto is 'Buy British.'
You've guessed by now I'm Mrs. Peep, for I can be no
other,
Yes, Bo-Peep is my only girl, and I'm her only mother.
They called me 'Bo' when quite a girl, that name it came
in handy,
The reason why they called me 'Bow' was because my
legs were bandy.
They said that I took after dad, when youth was in the
making,
But there was very little left when father did the taking.
My curly hair's been handed down, in fact it was an heir-
loom,
For mother found it in a box that she kept in the spare-
room.
Now girls if you would like some hints, I feel it is my duty
To tell you little things I know on woman's aid to beauty.
My dimples! ah, you envy those, they are a beauty sym-
bol,
I got those dents within my cheecks by sleeping on a
thimble.
My skin has got that glossy sheen that many think perfec-
tion,
I rub in oil with my palm and get schoolgirl's com-
plexion.
Should you be wanting shell-like ears, now don't go in
for squashing,
The best thing is to use great care and pin them back
when washing!
A rosebud mouth like mine, you know, can always be
acquired
Providing that you never gape when you are feeling tired.

161

With teeth I take the greatest care, of nothing I am prouder
For each night when I take them out, I scrub with emery powder.
Now here's a hint to wave your hair, it will also help to save it,
With hair untied—the tide goes out, and tides are sure to wave it.
If you want eyebrows nicely plucked here's an idea for them,
Rub on some cheese, then go to sleep, the mice will come and gnaw them.
And should you wish to red your lips the cheapest way to stripe them,
Is to eat a slice of bread and jam and then forget to wipe them.
The way to hide a shiny nose is often quite a puzzle,
If you find that powder doesn't do, then buy yourself a muzzle.
With face creams you should take great care, don't use the cream of tartar;
A little vitriol's very good—that'll make your face much smarter.
When you've a boil upon your neck you soon will be in clover,
If you put your neck upon the hob and let it boil over.
So write to me for 'free advice': just mark your letters 'Hostage'
Enclose your name and your address and two pounds ten for 'postage.'

(*Any comic song suitable for* Dame *can be introduced here, or the following may be used.*)

SONG

(*Air:* '*Our Lodger's such a nice young man.*')

If I could find a nice young man,
A nice young man who's free,
So tall—so strong,
To make a fuss of me.
I'd never let him leave me;

Oh dear—Oh dear no
I want a fine handsome looking man
Who looks like Romeo.
(Baron's *voice heard off singing, 'I hear you calling me.'*)

DAME: Oh! my prayers have been heard. (*Stands with eyes closed and arms wide apart.*) Come to my arms, my narcissus! In fact I don't mind if you are only a sweet william, so long as you'll be the flower of my heart. Yes, even a cauliflower.

(Baron *enters*)

(*He rushes into her arms. She opens her eyes.*)

DAME: Well I'm—Now a joke's a joke but you are no narcissus; why I've seen things like you on coconut trees.

BARON: Well, if it comes to that you're no buttercup.

DAME: But remember I am still surrounded with widow's weeds, with those removed my *heart's ease* would quickly flourish.

BARON: You don't want a lover, you want a jobbing gardener.

DAME: Well, I shouldn't engage you if I did. A fine mess you made of your own bit of garden. No wonder your potatoes were useless, you planted them so near to the spring onions that their eyes were full of tears.

BARON: Yes, and the onions were full of springs. What did you do in your own garden? You watered the celery with red ink and hoped it would come up rhubarb.

DAME: Don't be so *red-ink-ulas*. What did you do with those cornflowers you grew? Why you tried to make them into a blancmange.

BARON: Not so silly as you, anyhow—you buried a heap of cinders and thought it would come up coal.

DAME: Don't you talk so *fuelish*. I did nothing of the sort. I was only trying to make a cinder path for my *runner* beans.

BARON: My garden was the talk of the neighbourhood.

163

DAME: Yes, they all *talked* about it, but you wouldn't like to know what they said.

BARON: What's happened to your garden—it's all gone.

DAME: That wasn't my fault—a cat came and ate it all up.

BARON: But I say we musn't talk too much about *allotments*, hadn't we better talk about the *plot?*

DAME: I suppose we had. I wonder if you've seen my Bo-Peep anywhere about.

BARON: No. She is out somewhere minding my sheep, and woebetide her if any are missing when she returns home with them.

DAME: But surely you wouldn't be angry with the girl if she was a few short.

BARON: Surely she could count them.

DAME: Ah, that's it. You see the moment she sits on a stile and starts to count sheep she will drop off to sleep. It is a sure cure for insomnia. And if she did have forty winks she couldn't keep her eyes on the sheep.

BARON: But are you sure she could count them correctly while they were all running about?

DAME: Certainly. She counts how many legs she can see, then she divides the total by four and that gives her the number of sheep.

BARON: I tried that way of counting once and two of my sheep were running about on only three legs, so you see I was half a sheep short. It worried me so that I went and bought a couple of legs of mutton to make my flock complete.

DAME: (*Singing in style of yodel.*) You're a liarty—a liarty.

BARON: Don't you call me a liar'ty.

DAME: How could I, why I'm a perfect Lady.

BARON: If you say that, we must both be li—, I should say 'holy friars.'

164

DUET

(Air —'The Two Obadiahs'.)

BARON: Said one holy friar to the other holy friar,
Let us sing, holy friar, let us sing.

DAME: Said one holy friar to the other holy friar,
You begin, holy friar, you begin.

BARON: Said the one holy friar: 'the whole truth I will disclose
And from my *lips* I'll let you know a lie it never flows.'

DAME: Then that must be the reason that you talk so through
your nose.

BARON: Said the other holy friar that is true.

DAME: Said one holy friar to the other holy friar,
Now it's you, holy friar, now it's you.

BARON: Said one holy friar to the other holy friar,
That I knew, holy friar, that I knew.

DAME: I heard somebody mention that *my* singing was quite
nice.
And makes them think of angels singing up in Paradise.

BARON: That noise you make is not a voice, it's what they call
a *vice*.

DAME: Said the other holy friar: 'That is rude.'

BARON: Said one holy friar to the other holy friar,
'Let us try, holy friar, let us try,
Who can tell, holy friar, yes tell, holy friar,
The really best and biggest kind of lie.'

DAME: I knew a boy who grew so fast that when he was a youth,
They couldn't keep him in a house, his head pushed through
the roof.

BARON: I knew a politician once always spoke the truth.

DAME: You have won, holy friar, you have won.

(Dance and exeunt L.)

(*Sound of horn heard off* R. Boy Blue *enters with horn in hand.*)

BOY BLUE: Where can she be, my own, my precious dear,
My clarion note I'm sure she cannot hear. (*Looks off* R.)

(Nicadeem *enters* L. *He is disguised and carries a bundle of sticks.*)

NICADEEM: (*Aside.*) Boy Blue! My hated rival—the one who I
despise, but he will never know me while I'm in this disguise.

BOY BLUE: (*Turning.*) Why who are you?

NICADEEM: I am just a forest woodman, poor,
collecting bits of firewood to help my scanty store.

BOY BLUE: Perhaps you will be good enough to help me in my
quest,
And lead me to a country maid, the one that I love best.
A maiden fair of beauty rare, her name it is Bo-Peep,
She roams the woods here daily and tends the Baron's
sheep;
I have wandered many weary miles since quite the early
dawn
But still I can't discover yet the way that she has gone.

NICADEEM: (*Humbly.*) But I sire, can direct you to the path
the maiden took,
Go straight down by the winding lane then cross the bab-
bling brook,
Then take the narrow pathway that leads up to the hill,
And walk a little distance on until you reach the mill,
And when at last you come upon the entrance to the glade,
There beside the water mill you'll see your precious maid.

BOY BLUE: A thousand thanks! A thousand thanks—you are
indeed a friend,
To meet the treasure of my heart my way I'll quickly wend.

(*Runs off* L.)

(Nicadeem *gives a hoarse laugh of revenge as he speaks in tones of spite.*)

NICADEEM: Ha! Ha! Revenge is very sweet. I told the fool all
wrong,
That was not the path at all that Bo-Peep went along,
I saw her over yonder (*Pointing off R.*) in a meadow fast
asleep,
And while she slept I crept along and scattered all her
sheep.
Now when she wakes she'll be alarmed to find her flock not
there,
And doubtless she will soon be filled with anguish and des-
pair,
Then close up to this maiden's side I'll instantly appear,
And pour soft words of sympathy into her pretty ear,
And promise her, if she consents to be my loving bride,
To quickly find those missing sheep and bring them to her
side.
But no—on second thought, perhaps, I know what I will
do,
I'll tell her that the culprit was that hateful Boy in Blue.
I'll tell her that he was the one who stole her missing sheep,
And then the love she has for him no longer will she keep;
I'll go and tell the Baron first who caused the sheep to stray,
For he knows he can trust me and believe in what I say.

(*Looking off R.*)

But ah, Bo-Peep she comes this way, perhaps I'd better go
And get things right with the Baron and tell him all I know.

(*Exit L.*)

(*Chorus off stage R. sing following softly.*)

Little Bo-Peep has lost her sheep,
And can't tell where to find them,
Leave them alone and they'll come home
And bring their tails behind them.

(*Enter Bo-Peep R.*)

BO-PEEP: Oh dear! Oh dear! I'm so distressed my flock of
sheep are lost,
I must try and keep this secret from the Baron at all cost,
I've looked for them both near and far and by the babbling
brook

But still I've not discovered yet the pathway that they took,
I think while seated on the stile I must have gone to sleep,
And while I dozed somebody came and robbed me of my sheep,
But while I slept I had a dream—if only it were true,
And I could really be the bride of the one they call Boy Blue.
For then I'd have no fear at all if he were by my side,
The Baron he could do his worst and I'd be satisfied;
Although I'm grieved I've lost my sheep my thoughts they still remain
Of that romantic daydream with its beautiful refrain.

(The following can be sung by choir off stage or by Bo-Peep *herself.)*

SONG

(Air: 'Little Dolly Daydream.')

Just a little day dream,
Dreaming of my beau
The whole day through—my boy in Blue,
For you I have a heart that's beating true
And no one's going to win that heart but you.

(NOTE: *If the above is taken as a solo by* Bo-Peep, *it might be repeated by choir off stage while* Bo-Peep *gives a short dance.)*

(Exit R.)

(Enter Baron L. Bo-Peep *re-enters R.)*

BARON: And so I hear you've lost my sheep, you careless little hussy,
The news has made me mad with rage and sent my head all muzzy,
You careless wench, now list to me and tell without delay
How was it that you came to let my flock all go astray.

BO-PEEP: I fear they wandered from my side whilst I was in a doze,
For when I woke they all had gone—

168

BARON: Which very plainly shows—
That they had all been stolen by some good-for-nothing knave.
A lad who's known quite well to me—

BO-PEEP: Tell me his name I crave.

BARON: His name's Boy Blue—

BO-PEEP: It cannot be.

BARON: He is the thief I say
I heard it from a trusted friend whom I met on my way.

BO-PEEP: Say what you will—think what you may, but Boy Blue didn't do it.

BARON: If you stand there and doubt my word, I'll quickly make you rue it.
I'll tie him to the old oak tree beside my field of clover
And there I'll make your dear Boy Blue just *black* and blue all over.

(*Exit* Baron *in a rage R.*)

(*She is about to follow* Baron *off—speaks pleadingly.*)

BO-PEEP: Oh please don't strike my dear Boy Blue it wasn't he I swear it,
To hear a slur upon his name I really cannot bear it.
If any harm should come to him my aching heart will shatter,
Can no one help me in my grief?

(*Enter* Dame *L.*)

DAME: Why, darling, what's the matter?

BO-PEEP: Oh mother dear, my life's so sad I wish that I could end it;
I feel my heart is broken now.

DAME: Let's see if I can mend it.
I know what makes you feel so bad and now my one advice is,
Don't eat so many lollipops and those big tup'ny ices.

169

BO-PEEP: No, nother dear, it isn't that—it's the Baron's accusation,
He says that Boy Blue stole his sheep—

DAME: Oh what a fabrication!
Come tell me all about it, dear, here in this chilly climate,
But as I want to hear it quick you needn't stop to rhyme it.

BO-PEEP: Well, mother, it was like this, I was sitting on the old stile by Lover's Lane.

DAME: (*Romantically*) Ah that was where your dear father proposed to me. He looked into my eyes and popped the question—then he lifted me off the stile and popped his braces.

BO-PEEP: Well there I was, mother, minding the old Baron's sheep, when I think the heat of the sun must have sent me off to sleep.

DAME: Went to sleep in the day time. You should have done the same as your poor dear father did on hot days—he always wore a *wide-awake* hat.

BO-PEEP: Don't interrupt me, mother. And when I again opened my eyes all the sheep had gone.

DAME: And so the poor dog had none. How silly of me, I am in the wrong pantomime. That's Mother Hubbard. You say your sheep had gone.

BO-PEEP: Yes, they had all flown.

DAME: Don't talk such nonsense, child, sheep don't fly.

BO-PEEP: I mean they had all suddenly disappeared.

DAME: Sounds to me more like a conjuring trick. They must have all been 'Maskelyne' sheep.

BO-PEEP: But, mother, that's not all, I have other troubles to bear.

DAME: Don't tell me you lost your toffee apple as well.

BO-PEEP: No, mother, it is the thought that Boy Blue will be accused of being a thief.

170

DAME: Don't you worry, my dear, no one will believe it. Why Bloy Boo—er—I mean Boy Blue, he wouldn't rob a spider of his fly. You wait till I meet the Baron, I'll tell him just a few home facts about himself. I'll tell him he'd better mind his P's and Q's as well as his I. O. U.'s. (*She turns and meets* Baron *as he enters L.*)

BARON: Don't talk to me, I'm too upset, with anger I could weep,
That good-for-nothing girl of yours has lost my precious sheep.

DAME: Lost your sheep, what do you mean—your brain is in a whirl,
The truth is that your silly sheep have lost my darling girl,
The careless way you keep your sheep is where your method fails,
Why don't you have a little map just fastened on their tails.

BARON: I tell you Boy Blue stole those sheep, he led them through the thickets.

BO-PEEP: I say Boy Blue is straight and true

DAME: He never had the *rickets*.

BO-PEEP: Let us try and find the sheep, and then we can control them.

DAME: And then we all can ask each one just who it was who stole them.

TRIO

(*Air: 'Loch Lomond'.*)

BARON: You take the long road.

DAME: And I'll take the wrong road,

BO-PEEP: I'll go where I fancy I'll find them,

BARON: But what can we do not to let them stray again?

DAME: We must tie their adresses on behind them.

(*Short dance might be introduced here. All go off L.*)

(*Enter* Boy Blue *R.*)

BOY BLUE: I cannot find my sweet Bo-Peep, for hours I've
vainly tried,
I've tramped through ev'ry hill and dale throughout the
countryside,
But when we meet I wonder if I'd better tell the truth
Or let her think that I am just a humble country youth.
For if the truth she really knew 'twould cause her great sur-
prise,
When she finds out her Boy Blue is a real prince in disguise.
If only I could get advice as to what I'd better do,
If someone could befriend me now——

(Fairy *comes from behind tree.*)

FAIRY: What help can I give you?

BOY BLUE: Oh! really it's so good of you to come here
to my aid, But who are you?

FAIRY: A Fairy, sire, who lives within the glade,
You want advice I heard you say—you seem to be in doubt,
But will you not confide in me?

BOY BLUE: If you will help me out.
But first I'd better let you know that I am deep in love
With a maiden who has features like the angels up above.
Her name's Bo-Peep.

FAIRY: I know it all—and you are her Boy Blue.
I'll tell to you a secret now—she's much in love with you.

BOY BLUE: But are you sure?

FAIRY: Indeed I am, I hear her day by day,
Speaking of her love for you as she goes by this way,
From in my secret hiding place I watch all passers by,
And do my best to warn them if real danger should be nigh.
For you I have a message——

BOY BLUE: For me—oh, can I guess?
It's all about my sweetheart and our future happiness.

FAIRY: Oh no, you're wrong—there's someone who

172

has played a wicked game
And is trying hard to do his best to brand your honest
name.

BOY BLUE: What can it mean—please tell me now—

FAIRY: I'll make my message brief,
The rumour that has reached my ears has named *you* as a
thief.

BOY BLUE: What! me a thief? It is not true—I am an
honest man.

FAIRY: Of course you are, and that is why I'll help you all
I can,
The baron thinks you stole the sheep that poor Bo-Peep has
lost,
But I will put this matter right, I will at any cost.
Come, take my crook down yonder and wave it o'er the
brook,
And quickly it will indicate the road the lost sheep took.
And soon you'll find they'll all return as quickly as they
strayed——

BOY BLUE *(Taking crook)*: Oh, how can I thank you enough
for your most kindly aid?

FAIRY: Pray hurry! You've no time to waste—that crook will
lose its power
If you don't exercise your wish within one golden hour.

BOY BLUE: But once again my gratitude I really must express,
And I will go, good Fairy, now.

FAIRY: I wish you all success.

(Fairy *makes exit behind tree.* Boy Blue *is about to Exit L.
when he is met by* Bo-Peep.)

BOY BLUE: Ah sweetheart mine, you're here at last, I feared
that I should miss you,
And so my dreams have now come true, for in my dreams
I kissed you.

BO-PEEP: But dreams go by the contrary, so that can never be.

173

BOY BLUE: If that's the case it's simplified—it means *you* just kiss *me*.

BO-PEEP: This is not time to talk of love. I'm in such sad distress,
   I'm told my sheep were stolen by a scoundrel—can you guess?

BOY BLUE: I've heard it all and I can prove that tale is quite untrue.
   You thought I was the culprit then?

BO-PEEP: No. I knew it wasn't you.
   But what is that—a fairy crook you carry in your hand?

BOY BLUE: The magic power that it has is now at my command,
   Two wishes it will grant to me—two wishes, nothing more,
   The first shall be that all your sheep it quickly shall restore.

BO-PEEP: To clear your name must be your next—

BOY BLUE: That quickly shall be done,
   But that will end my wishes—how I'd like another one.

BO-PEEP: What is the other wish you seek?

BOY BLUE: What is it—can't you guess?
   I wish that you would say the word to make my happiness.

BO-PEEP: You want no wand to answer that quite plainly you should see,

BOY BLUE: I wonder who I'd better ask?

BO-PEEP: That question rests with *me*.

BOY BLUE: I feel as I gaze in your eyes your answer I can guess.

BO-PEEP: What do my eyes appear to say?

BOY BLUE: They plainly answer yes—
   Of happiness I now am sure—a life of perfect bliss,
   So let us sing our cares away and seal it with a kiss.

(Any simple love duet can be introduced here. Something of

the 'If you were the only girl in the World' type of number. At finish of duet they exeunt R.)

*(*Nicadeem *enters L. He shakes his fist at* Bo-Peep *and* Boy Blue *as they go off.)*

NICADEEM: Curse that boy—he's won the prize I tried so hard to win,
But when she hears he stole the sheep some trouble may begin,
The Baron he believes my word, he does not know the truth,
For now he thinks that young Boy Blue a real dishonest youth.
If I can make Bo-Peep think that, my plans will all be set,
And I shall triumph in the end and win my sweetheart yet.
I'll go and listen to their plans and patiently I'll wait
And tell them both just what I know—I'll do it *now—*

*(*Fairy *enters from behind tree.)*

FAIRY: Too late!

NICADEEM: What you again—get back I say—you cannot frighten me
I'll let you know this game is mine—I'm going to win.

FAIRY: We'll see.

*(*Fairy *makes exit behind tree.)*

(Exit Nicadeem *R.)*

(Enter Baron *L.)*

BARON: Everything is going wrong—my flock cannot be found,
Though I have scoured the countryside for miles and miles around.

*(*Dame *heard singing off stage L.)*

BARON: Ah, what is that strange noise I hear—it makes my flesh all creep.

(Enter Dame *L.)*

DAME: I'm glad you like my singing.

BARON: I thought it was my sheep.

DAME: Your ewes can't sing they only *baa,* especially if the
ewe's sick.

BARON: There's nothing very strange in that, there's always
'bars' in music.

DAME: I've never heard of music yet that sounds the least bit
sheepy,
Although the *'Tales* of Hoffmann' have at times made
me feel sleepy.

BARON: Those *tails* of the 'Bark-arole' to me seem rather
doggy,
So your voice could round up my sheep some evening when
it's foggy.

DAME: When I was young my voice you know was quite a
soft soprano,
It sounds much harder now it's set.

BARON: A set they call Meccano,
I've no doubt I can sing as well although I've never tried it.

DAME: Well, let us sing a short duet and then we can decide it.

BARON: What shall we sing?

DAME: Oh I don't mind—try something that's
beguiling.
Suppose we sing 'Hail Smiling Morn' and see who does the
smiling.

*(They prepare to sing duet. Dame hands Baron
sheet of music.)*

DAME: Here's the very thing. I got this bit of music this morning,
It came from the butcher's with the cat's lights in.

BARON: Yes, 'Hail Smiling Morn' is a fine song.

DAME: I used to sing it when I was a child.

BARON: Was it written as long ago as that? What key shall we
sing it in?

176

DAME: I don't mind. It being a song of the early morning why not try it in 'Par*key*'. It's always very parky in the early morn.

BARON: Give me the note. *(Dame sounds note.)* That key is 'Hus*key*.' Shall we harmonise?

DAME: No, that always makes me bilious.

BARON: What *do* you mean? Don't you know what I mean by 'harmonise'?

DAME: Of course I do—it's that stuff they put on wedding cakes.

BARON: Nothing of the sort. To 'harmonise' means to make a noise like a harmonium.

DAME: Well I knew it was something to do with weddings. Go on you start.

BARON: *(Singing)* 'Ail Smiling Morn—Smiling——

DAME: No, no. You've dropped the aitch in 'hail'. You said 'Ale'—this is not a drinking song.

BARON: I don't know so much about that—look, it's published by Boosey & Co.

DAME: Now start with me. *(Sings.)* Hail Smiling Morn—Smiling— *(Stops singing.)*

BARON: I can't quite understand 'the hail makes the morning smile.' I suppose when it snows the morning screams with delight.

DAME: It is not that sort of hail at all. This is the hail that means I am pleased to meet you.

BARON: I see, a sort of Hailo (Hullo) Smiling Morn.

DAME: *(Singing.)* Hail Smiling Morn—Smiling Morn—Smiling Morn.

BARON: That's three mornings gone already—so here we are at Thursday.

DAME: Yes, and if you don't hurry up the whole week will have gone. *(Singing)* Hail Smiling Morn.

BARON:*(Singing.)*Goodlaughternoon—laughternoon—laughternoon.

DAME: What nonsense.

BARON: Why shouldn't the afternoon do a bit of smiling as well?

DAME: But this is essentially a *morning* song.

BARON: Well don't sing any more or all your relations will be in *mourning,* and there'll be a little headstone erected to your memory on which the words will be written 'Shot at Dawn'—smiling dawn.

DAME: But who will do the shooting?

BARON: *I* will.

> *(This burlesque singing of 'Hail Smiling Morn'*
> *can be extended to any length required.)*

DAME: I'm sorry if you do not care to hear my little canto.

BARON: No, I think you'd better stop your song and get on with the panto:
Now let me see how far were we when you commenced your shrieking?

DAME: Why where the sheep had gone astray that everyone was seeking,
You'd said that Boy Blue stole the sheep.

BARON: That was the boy who did it.

DAME: Don't you dare say that again—remember I forbid it.

BARON: It seems to me you love that boy. Don't worry, I'm not jealous.

DAME: I say he did *not* steal those sheep.

BARON: Who was it then—come tell us.

DAME: Quite who it was I do not know—'twas someone

178

I'd be loathing,
A kind of wicked human wolf who dresses in sheep's cloth-
ing.

BARON: I'd like to get my fist well clenched, then on his nose
impress it.

DAME: Who could have done that wicked deed?

(Nicadeem *rushes on and stands with bowed head.*)

NICADEEM: I'm guilty. I confess it.

(Dame *makes a rush at him about to strike him.*
Baron *holds her back.*)

DAME: So he's the cause of all this strife. I always did dislike him.

BARON: I feel I'd like to dot him one—

(Fairy *enters from behind tree.*)

FAIRY: One moment. Do not strike him.
Though lots of deeds I know he's done you mortals have re-
sented,
But *I* went to his aid as well, and now he has repented.

NICADEEM: I vow in future I'll go straight, from now until my
ending,

DAME: And remember you will hear from me if I should catch
you bending.

BARON: Here comes Boy Blue and Bo-Peep too; into her eyes
he's gazing.

DAME: Oh, Baron, won't you look in mine—the effect is
quite amazing.

(Baron *and* Dame *gaze at one another romantically.*)

(*Enter* Boy Blue *and* Bo-Peep *R.*)

BOY BLUE: *(Turns to* Nicadeem.*)* What you here
still—you——

DAME: No, Boy Blue—I beg you don't chastise
him,

He's quite good now. He's so reformed you'll hardly recognise him,
He'd always been a naughty lad from the day his mother breeched him.
though once the black sheep of the flock the Fairy now has bleached him.

BO-PEEP: *(Indicating* Boy Blue.*)* Mother, dear, we are betrothed—
This is my secret lover.
And there's another secret too you shortly will discover,
Mother—Baron—listen all—'twill be a big surprise,
When you all learn that Boy Blue is a *real* Prince in disguise.

BARON: A Prince!

DAME: Oh dear! oh dear! now we shall have a castle,
(to Bo-Peep.*)* In future, dear, you must not bring your fish home in a parcel.

BARON: As matrimony's in the air I suppose we'd better do it.

DAME: Oh take me for your 'awful' wife—I'm sure you'll never rue it.

NICADEEM: But what of me?

BARON: Now you've reformed I'll have you as my valet.

DAME: And if you don't behave yourself I'll coax you with a mallet.

BOY BLUE: I invite you all to dine to-night within my stately Palace.
(To Nicadeem.*)* I invite you, too, to join us there to show I bear no malice.

BO-PEEP: My thanks to you, dear Fairy, too, for making good of evil.

DAME: *(Dancing with joy.)* I'll do a little dance for joy—I feel a perfect de-vil.

FAIRY: I've only done what fairies should, and let this be

180

recorded,
Throughout your lives you'll always find true virtue is rewarded.

BARON: I've found my sheep—I've found a wife—*(To* Dame*)*
May I call you Aggie?

DAME: And you will find *this* little lamb will never turn out
scraggy.

*(*Bo-Peep *and* Boy Blue *advance.)*

BO-PEEP: We one and all are happy now and every heart re-
joices,
So Prince Boy Blue will blow his horn to call the fairy
voices.

*(*Boy Blue *blows horn. The following to be sung by
all on stage and also by choir off stage.)*
FINALE

Little Bo-Peep has found her sheep,
So now is the time for laughter.
May she and Boy Blue, with their love so true,
Live happily ever after.

CURTAIN.

»

THE SLEEPING BEAUTY

(1948)

CHARACTERS:
King
Queen
Witch
Prince
Fairy
Father Time
Sleeping Beauty
Small Troupe of Fairy Dancers (optional)

SCENE: Interior of King's palace. Coloured draperies, to open in centre. Side wings to represent, if possible, pillars. Gilded pedestals up back, and anything to convey grandeur.

Dancers enter to light music and give short dance. At finish of dance, Fairy enters.

FAIRY: Today shall be a day of joy, for let it now be told,
The baby princess, whom we love, is now just one year old.
So one and all come gaze upon this precious tiny tot,
I wave my wand, and now behold (*Curtains up back open showing royal cot containing large doll*) our princess in her cot.
With all our hearts we wish her joy, health, wealth and happiness
And may her beauty never wane—our dearly loved princess.
So let us dance around her now on this her natal day
You are one and all invited—

(*Sound of siren whistle is heard off stage. Witch enters carrying besom broom.*)

WITCH: I'm here.

183

FAIRY: Please go away.

WITCH: What's that I hear? you don't want me. I'm left out in
the cold;
I suppose you all despise me just because I'm getting old.

FAIRY: It's not your age that I despise. I love the old and frail,
But witches, I have understood, bring curses in their trail.
So now begone.

WITCH: But don't forget, I'll give you tit for tat,
One day a curse I'll put upon that little royal brat,
You all will live to rue this day that you have angered me,
A witch's curse you'll never thwart, remember that—

FAIRY: We'll see.

(*Siren whistle heard off. Exit* Witch.)

FAIRY: Come fairies all, we know no fear, as all good fairies
should;
For we are sent upon this earth to cheer and help do good.
Let's sing unto the young princess, while she's in sweet repose,
May dream she is in fairyland though tucked beneath the
clothes.

(*Dancers advance toward cot, gather round and sing a lullaby.
The following may be used:
'Alabama Coon.'*)

Hush-a-by you precious royal baby,
Pretty little girlie full of charm,
Hush-a-by—don't you cry
Sweet princess of beauty
The fairies here will keep you from all harm.

(*Short dance. Curtain up back close. All dance off.*)
(*Enter* King *and* Queen.)

QUEEN: Oh Kingie dear, now do you know where our best gold-
en tray is?

KING: What do you want with golden trays?

QUEEN: Don't you know what to-day is?

KING: I think it must be *Thirstday*, for I've got an awful thirst, dear,

QUEEN: Why, it's our dear baby's birthday

KING: of course, it is her first, dear.

But she can't sit upon a tray, as an *entree* she'd look wonky

QUEEN: I want it for her cake, you ass

KING: Well there, I am a donkey.

QUEEN: If we don't have a birthday cake 'twill cause a lot of scandal,
I'll get one from Genoa.

KING: Yes, with one big Roman candle.

QUEEN: A Roman candle on her cake! With fright 'twould send her hair up

KING: 'Twould celebrate our *golden reign*, and cause a reg'lar flare up.

QUEEN: Our darling babe *must* have a cake, and one that looks enticing

KING: With lots of *Pa's* and *Ma'sipan*, and covered up with icing.

QUEEN: We haven't time to get all that and get it here by tea time,

KING: But can't you make a cake yourself?

QUEEN: I haven't got much free time.
But somehow we must get a cake for our darling one might—
Not think her birthday very bright.

KING: Why not a cake of 'Sunlight?'

QUEEN: I'll send round to the baker's dear, and see if he's a *round* cake.

KING: When he knows it's for a *sovereign* he will surely send a *pound* cake.

That settles that. And now, my dear, just who are we inviting?
We want to keep our party nice without bad words or fighting.

QUEEN: Who shall we ask?

KING: Don't ask me. *You* know the neighbours better.

QUEEN: There's Mrs. Flucome and her quads—on no account forget her.
With all her four dear baby boys 'they'll cheer our young *Princess* up.

KING: But 'spose she can't tell which is which, my word there'll be a *mess* up.
You send our invitations out on paper we have crested.
Just say 'At our big birthday treat your *presents* are requested.'

QUEEN: Now how about our darling child, our baby we're ignoring,
I wonder if she's still asleep.

KING: I thought I heard her snoring.

(*They both tip-toe up to back and peep through curtains.*)

QUEEN: Oh look, the dear one's fast asleep—how sweet she looks—

KING: Yes, rather.

QUEEN: She likes her bottle, doesn't she?

KING: How like her dear old father.

(Queen *picks baby up in her arms.*)

QUEEN: The little darling knows her Pa. She never makes a blunder

KING: Yes, everytime she sees my face she starts to laugh—

QUEEN: No wonder.

KING: (*Tickling baby's face*) Kitchie-kitchie-kutchie koo.

(Sound of baby crying off stage.)

QUEEN: She has now commenced her whin*ees.*

KING: She may not like my 'Kitchie-koos', she thinks I'm talking Chinese.
Put the darling back in bed—her bottle let her suck in.

QUEEN: The little precious wants her food.

KING: *(Indicating bed)* Well give her a good tuck in.

(Queen places baby back in cot.)

KING: I'll sing our baby girl to sleep, if I can get the right air.

QUEEN: Don't *you* start singing to her, dear, she'll think she's got the nightmare.

(Song. Air: 'Annie Rooney.')

QUEEN: A pretty face—a tiny nose

KING: Dimpled cheeks—ten tiny toes

QUEEN: Her tie—ups made with pretty bows
Has little Princess Beauty.

KING: And ev'ry time say 'Goo-goo'
Her blue eyes seem to look me through
Then tries to say 'The same to you'
Does little Princess Beauty.

(Refrain.)
(They let curtains close.)

QUEEN: She's my baby—I'm her Ma,

KING: She's *my* baby—I'm her Pa.

QUEEN: Don't you worry
Never we'll part

BOTH: Little Princess Beauty she is *our* sweetheart.

(Optional dance and Exeunt.)
(Siren whistle heard off. Witch *enters. She looks about.)*

187

WITCH: No fairies here—that is well,
   I've come to plan my threatened spell
   I'll give those pretty nymphs a shock,
   They shan't make me their laughing stock,
   I'll lead them all a pretty dance,
   When for revenge I get my chance
   I'll fill them all with deadly fears,
   If I've to wait for years and years
   (*Peeps into curtains up back*)
   On you, you little brat I vow
   I'll have revenge.
   (*Cry of baby heard*) Oh, stop that row.

(*Siren whistle heard.* Witch *hurries off giving fiendish laugh.*)

(*Fairy music. Cry of baby is heard. Dancers enter. They carry large cake, with one electric light on top to represent candle. The cake is placed C. of stage, they dance around.*
The cake could be made in sections to suggest portions of cake, each dancer might take up portion, to which a ribbon is attached, and lead into a kind of maypole dance. The following might be used for vocal number.)

(*Air: 'Cold and Frosty Morning.'*)

Here we come wishing you joy to-day,
         Joy to-day
         Joy to-day,
May all your future be bright and gay
In spite of the Witch's warning.

(*Final dance and all exit.*)

(*Front tabs close. If this is not possible all lights out.* Father Time *enters. He carries an hour-glass in which a small electric light is fixed, giving just enough light to illuminate his face. Note —This part could easily be played by the* King. *The heavy disguise of the long flowing wig and beard would not be detected.*)

FATHER TIME: Fly each day in quick succession,
   I have time at my command,

188

Now the years are quickly fleeting
Fastly runs the golden sand.
Eighteen years have gone before us,
Since our Princess was in arms,
Years have added to her beauty
Time has but enhanced her charm.
Now her infant days are ended
Life to her brings something new
Time has brought love to this maiden
As I am sure she'll bring to you.

(*Exit* Father Time.)

(*All lights up. Full stage. Dancers enter. They back on to stage,
bowing as they move towards opposite side, singing as they
advance.*)

(*Song. Air: 'My Hero.'*)

ALL: Wel-come! wel-come to Beauty,Welcome to you;
    We're all wishing you gladness,
    And love that's true;
    May your future be bright, dear;
    Health, wealth with years of delight, dear;
    May Heaven bless.
    Wel-come! Wel-come to Beauty
    Welcome Princess.

(Beauty *enters. Comes down stage C.*)

BEAUTY: Thank you for your kindly greeting,
    Such loyalty I'm proud to see.
    Though the years are quickly fleeting
    You remain still true to me.
    Though I've Princess for my title,
    From true royal stock I came,
    Remember this—for it is vital
    I'm just a girl—we're *all* the same.

(*Dancers make their exit during her last two lines.*)

Always waiting for to-morrows,
When my hero I may find,
Someone who may end my sorrows;

Someone for my heart designed.
If I could but find a lover
To answer to my ardent prayer:
If but one I could discover,
Just my loving heart to share.

(*She turns about to make her exit, when the voice of the* Prince *is heard off. He sings a short verse of a love ballad. She stops and listens appearing greatly impressed. She looks off stage in the direction of voice.*)

A poor wandering minstrel. Dare I ask him in? (*Speaking off stage hesitatingly*) Er—will you come this way, please?

(*Enter* Prince. *He is dressed as a troubadour. He has a guitar slung across his back, and a small black mask covering his eyes. He bows to* Beauty *as he enters.*)

PRINCE: Did you call me, maiden fair?

BEAUTY: It was wrong I know—but there—
Was something in your charming voice
That made my lonely heart rejoice.

PRINCE: A thousand thanks. For I'm a poor—
And humble wand'ring troubadour.
Such praise is rare, I must confess
From one so high—a fair princess.

BEAUTY: I've sometimes wished that I might be
A person of no high degree,
And free to rove this world alone
And find a lover of my own.

PRINCE: Fear not, princess, the time will be
When you will know love's ecstasy,
Farewell, princess I wander on.

(Prince *bows low as he makes his exit.*)

BEAUTY: Alas, my manly hero's gone.
Had I been one of humble sphere,
My heart's desire would conquer here.

(Beauty *to sing any love ballad. At end of same she slowly makes her exit.*)

190

(*Siren whistle heard off.* Witch *enters.*)

WITCH: I've waited now for many a year,
But now the time is drawing near—
To carry out my cherished threats;
To fill them all with sad regrets.
(*Rubs her hands with glee*)
I'll start my plans without delay,
But ah! the King he comes this way.

(*Siren whistle heard off.* Witch *makes quick exit.*)
(King *enters, he is followed by the* Queen.)

KING: There's one thing dear that must be done, it's no good overlooking.

QUEEN: And pray what is it *must be done?*

KING: Why don't you know? Your cooking.

QUEEN: I'm sure where cooking is concerned I can always hold my head up.

KING: My dear, you know I'm underfed, that's why I get so fed up.

QUEEN: *You* underfed, I do *not* think. Your medical adviser
Always speaks about you as a perfect gormandiser.

KING: Well anyway each bill for food, I always have to foot it.

QUEEN: Although you pay for what you eat, I can't think where you put it.
Nine eggs for breakfast every day.

KING: Well, nothing could be finer,
Those eggs are always much too hard. They must be made in China.

QUEEN: What else have you to grumble at?

KING: Well, while we're on this matter,
I wish you'd buy chickens dear that are a little fatter.
That one for lunch was very flat.

QUEEN: But it came straight up from Dorset.

KING: Praps it travelled up by road and a lorry ran across it.

QUEEN: You always have Sir Loin of Beef—I think good meat is vital.

KING: If what we have is called *Sir* Loin, it must have lost its title.

QUEEN: When we have game you grumble too. I know no wife who'd house a—
Man like you who will complain. With grouse you are a grouser.
My tipsy cakes I know are good. The flavour almost stifles
You must admit *they* are all right.

KING: I never talk on *trifles*.
The muffin that I had for tea was hard—I had to hump it.

QUEEN: Oh, you're got muffins on the brain.

KING: You mean I'm off my crumpet.

QUEEN: I do my best, I can't do more and all I cook is eaten,
So, please, don't call your wife to book.

KING: The book you want is Beeton.

(Queen *sits and takes out knitting*.)

QUEEN: Now what is really wrong with you, you're getting a dyspeptic,
You want to eat your food with care.

KING: Or else with antiseptic.

QUEEN: It's ill-behaved to talk of food when we have others present.

KING: I hope I may get *well* behaved and soon be convalescent.

QUEEN: The more I work the less you're pleased. You're quite a paradox, dear,
(*Indicating knitting*) I even knit your woolly hose.

KING: I admit you give me *socks* dear.

192

The last pair that you made for me were rather shapeless clumpers,
They started off by being socks, then ended up as jumpers.

QUEEN: About my work you're most unkind, you make remarks most horrid,
At times you truly cause me pain.

KING: That's why you knit your forehead.

QUEEN: I've been a real true wife to you.

KING: Of course you have, my Queenie.

QUEEN: To you I'm anything but Queen, you treat me like a Tweeny.

KING: Oh no, my dear, I love my Queen, I never provoke her,
You are the best in all the pack, while I am just the Joker.

QUEEN: It's twenty years since I wed you—I oft think now I blundered.

KING: Have we been married twenty years? It seems more like a hundred.

QUEEN: In dreams I see my wedding day, and all my bridal make-up.

KING: To me it also seems a dream and I try not to wake up.

QUEEN: That day you gave your heart and hand. We then were gay and youthful,
And now you don't give me a thought.

KING: My dear, now do be truthful,
I think of you the whole day long.

QUEEN: You think as very *few* think.

KING: I tell you dear I think of you. I won't say what I *do* think.

QUEEN: My ermine coat I've had for years, it's really most revolting,
The fur can hardly now be seen—

KING: It may be that it's moulting.

193

QUEEN: What do you ever give to me? No wonder neighbours slight us.

KING: Don't forget I kissed you once and gave you laryngitis.

QUEEN: I have a birthday coming on, I soon shall start collecting,
For I shall then expect a gift—

KING: All right go on expecting.

QUEEN: So now we'll sing a short duet. They must expect one from us,
And we will tell them what we'll give and carry out our promise.

DUET
(Air: 'A Little Bit Off the Top.')

QUEEN: When I got married to you, my dear,
    Long years ... ago,

KING: You promise to share your life with me
    In weal ... and woe,

QUEEN: You *woes* I don't mind sharing, its your *wheels* I do not like
    For all day long I ride on a rusty bike:

KING: When I got married to you, my dear,
    A wife . . . I took,

QUEEN: What did you think you were going to get?

KING: A good . . . plain cook.

QUEEN: I cook your meals with greatest care, the best I can produce,

KING: I must admit you have certainly cooked my goose.

QUEEN: When I got married to you, my dear,
    You made . . . a vow
    You'd never keep me up late at night
    Like you . . . do now.

194

KING: The hours I keep are *early* ones, with this you must
    agree
For when I get home it's usually after three.

When I got married to you, my dear,
You looked . . . so sweet,
So tender, dainty and elegant;
So trim . . . and neat.

QUEEN: You said you could devour me, with love you were so
    mad.

KING: I felt that I could eat you then, and now I wish I had.

QUEEN: When I got married to you, my dear,
Our mothers . . . cried,
As they were standing in the church
Both side . . . by side,
My mother cried her eyes out at the thought of losing me.

KING: And my mother cried for me just out of sympathy.

(*Optional dance and exeunt.*)
(*Siren whistle heard off.* Witch *enters with spinning-wheel un-*
der her cloak.)

WITCH: Alone once more, I'll now proceed
    To carry out my ruthless deed,
    I'll send that Princess in a trance
    And lead those fairy nymphs a dance,
    Ha! ha! I'll quickly let them see
    They can't do what they like with me
    The Princess comes—

(Beauty *enters*)

BEAUTY: Why, who are you?

WITCH: An old friend, darling, good and true.

BEAUTY: (*Seeing spinning-wheel*) What's that?

WITCH: A spinning-wheel, my dear.

BEAUTY: What is it for? It does look queer.

195

WITCH: True love together it will bind
   As you will very quickly find.

BEAUTY: How does it work? I'd like to know,

WITCH: Come closer and I'll quickly show.

   (Beauty *sits and starts to work wheel.*)

WITCH: Now guide the flax with your dear hand
   And very soon you'll understand.
   Now place your little finger so
   And let the wheel quite freely go.

BEAUTY: (*Works wheel. She screams*) Oh!

   (Witch *turns and rubs her hands with glee.*)

WITCH: What have you done, my pretty one?

BEAUTY: My finger's pricked!

WITCH: The deed is done.
   Revenge is mine! I've cast the spell

   You'll sleep to wake no more. Farewell!
            (*Siren whistle heard off. Exit* Witch.)

BEAUTY: A feeling strange comes over me,
   My eyes are growing dim,
   It's getting dark, I cannot see,
   My head begins to swim,
   I think I'll lay me down and rest,
   And sleep till early morn,
   And dream of one that I love best,
   My lover who has gone.

(*Curtains up back open. There, in place of the cot, is couch of
bright colour.* Beauty *lies down. Soft music for* Fairy *and*
Dancers' *entrance. They sing a lullaby, or the following may be
used.*)
      (*Air: 'Sing Me to Sleep.'*)

FAIRY: Sleep, Beauty, sleep and have no fear,

196

We'll not forget our Princess dear,
We will protect you from all harm,
Sleep will enhance our Beauty's charm.
Sleep, Beauty, sleep your long sleep through,
Sweet happy dreams will soon come to you,
If you are kissed by one you hold dear,
Waking you'll find that he is near.

(*Fairies dance off. Curtains close. All lights out.* Father Time
enters, as before.)

FATHER TIME: Our Beauty's doomed to sleep eternal
Through that wicked Witch's will,
Time will not decline her beauty,
She will keep her beauty still.
Perhaps some day when she awakens
From the couch on which she's lain,
Ardent love she may encounter
When she sees the light again.

(*Exit* Father Time. *All lights on.* Prince *enters, still in the guise
of a troubadour.*)

PRINCE: Where can she be, my   lovely Princess,
She won my heart, I must confess,
For years I've waited, but in vain,
In hopes of seeing her again.
Her beauty haunts me night and day
What e'er I do, where e'er I stray.
The fairies tell me to proceed
And seek for her—I should succeed.
I'll sing my song that she may hear
My voice, perchance, may bring her near.

(Prince *sings a few lines of his previous song. Curtains up back
slowly open.* Beauty *is seen there, sleeping.*)

Those features fair! Those hands so white,
Tis she! My love! My heart's delight!
Those fairies' words have all come true,
For they have guided me to you.
Those crimson lips I can't resist,
I must! I will (*Kisses her*)
　　　　Those lips I've kissed.

(*Enter* King. *He gazes in surprise at* Prince. *He assumes anger.*
Beauty *moves her arms, showing signs of awaking. Incidental
music, such as 'Awake,' might be played softly during the following few lines of dialogue.*)

KING: Who's this, within my palace grand—a common troubadour,
   If you don't get from here at once I'll let you know what for.

PRINCE: But sire, I've done a noble deed, for yonder if you
   glance,
   You'll see your lovely daughter has awakened from her trance.

(King *turns and sees* Beauty.)

KING: What's that! I can't believe my eyes! my daughter, Heaven bless her.

(King *rushes and embraces* Beauty.)

Would you like a cup of tea, my dear, there's one down on
   the dresser.
Oh, won't your mother dear be pleased. My word I am delighted.

(King *turns and goes up to* Prince.)

I nearly kissed the troubadour, I'm getting so excited.
I'll tell the glad news to the town and all the people in it.
I say, young man, don't go away, I'll be back in a minute.

(King *rushes off.*)

BEAUTY: What does this mean? We two alone. My noble troubadour.

PRINCE: It means that one true lover's kiss awakened you once
   more,
   'Twas I who gave that kiss to you.

BEAUTY: Twas you? What have you done?

PRINCE: I've also vowed that our two hearts must now just beat
   as one.

BEAUTY: But you are but a troubadour, while I'm of high
   degree,

198

Such things the state will not allow. It matters not to me.

PRINCE: But do you love me for myself?

BEAUTY: I do

PRINCE: Then let me tell—
The truth (Prince *removes mask*)
I'm a descendant from a monarchy as well.
I am Prince Hal, at your command. (*Bows*)

BEAUTY: Then why that strange disguise?

PRINCE: That I might prove the love was true from one I idolize.

(*They embrace. Any love duet can be introduced here. At finish of duet,* King *enters quickly. He is followed by the* Queen. *They come down stage and speak aside.*)

KING: Come see, my dear, our daughter wakes.

QUEEN: But who's that swell young pup, dear?

KING: He is the one who made her wake—a sort of knocker-up, dear,
In truth he is a troubadour.

QUEEN: A troubadour? How humble.

KING: Well, never mind, see what he's done, so you've no need to grumble.

QUEEN: You tell him now to get along

KING: Or more politely, hop it!

QUEEN: He's asking her a question now

KING: Perhaps he's going to pop it.

(Queen *goes up and speaks to* Prince.)

QUEEN: We've no room here for troubadours, so will you kindly leave us.

PRINCE: Your Majesty, I am a prince.

KING: Then why did you deceive us?

PRINCE: And now I ask your daughter's hand. I hope I've your permission.

KING: I freely give my daughter's hand, and her too in addition.

QUEEN: So now our daughter is betrothed there's nothing else to settle.

KING: I hope the Prince will stay to tea.
(*To* Queen) Get out the copper kettle.

BEAUTY: And so I haven't dreamed in vain. The past I still recall.

PRINCE: But now true happiness has come. True love has conquered all.

KING: (*To* Queen) My dear, we'd better celebrate.

QUEEN: Now stop your wild vagaries.

KING: We'll send the invitations out, and don't forget the Fairies.
(King *looks off stage*) Ah, here they are, Now come along
(Fairy *enters followed by dancers*)
                   let's dance the light fantastic,
My limbs aren't supple as they were, they want some new elastic.

QUEEN: On with the dance.

(*Siren whistle is heard off. They all shrink back in fear.*)

BEAUTY: The Witch! The Witch!

FAIRY: Don't fear, princess, we fairies are too clever,
You'll never see that Witch again—we've banished her for ever.

QUEEN: Well, now let's sing a merry lay, with aid of the orchestra.

(King *takes up a comic bouquet from over footlights and hands it to* Queen.)

KING: A bouquet for you

QUEEN: Don't be an ass, it's off an aspidistra.
  I've had my say—

KING: You always do, but now our story's ending.

BEAUTY: (*To audience*) I hope you'll all remember us
  When homeward you are wending.

PRINCE: I've won the prize for which I sought.

FAIRY: And I just did my duty.

KING: You now can all go home to bed
        Just like—

BEAUTY: The Sleeping Beauty.

FINALE

(*Any popular bright song of the moment to be introduced
here, following a few bars of the 'Wedding March.'*)

»
THE QUEEN OF HEARTS

(1948)

CHARACTERS:
King
Queen
Knave
Fairy Queen
Princess
Valentine
Yellow Dwarf
Witch
Two Courtiers

} If possible to be dressed after the style of picture playing cards

SCENE: Outside the King's Palace.

Half Lights   Tremolo music

Enter Witch

WITCH: To practise witchcraft is my aim—my mind is set on malice,
So I am here to place a curse upon the royal palace.
The royal Queen must be dethroned, also her kingly master,
And I shall work with all my will to bring them to disaster.
My curses are upon them all, although it is not known there,
For my plan is to put the Yellow Dwarf upon the throne there.
He'll furnish me with all I need and I shall then look smarter,
When he has wed the young Princess by special royal charter.

(Tremolo music stops. Witch *is about to make exit L. Enter* Fairy Queen *R. Lights up)*

FAIRY QUEEN: One moment—stay! You wretched witch. I'll see your plans are thwarted.

WITCH: I've got no time for fairy queens—I'd like the lot transported.

203

The Yellow Dwarf is fit to reign, so why should *you* resent it?

FAIRY QUEEN: Because I hate such evil things—I've come here to prevent it.

WITCH: I'll put my curses on you all if my plans are frustrated.

FAIRY QUEEN: I think your powers for doing harm are somewhat overrated.

WITCH: *You* have no powers compared with mine. The spells I cast are greater,
I tell you I am out to win.

FAIRY QUEEN: You will learn your answer later.

(Exit Witch. Fairy Queen *retires to side of stage while centre-piece is being turned)*

INTERIOR

So now I'll call the Royal pack—let them assemble here;
Ah! here we have the Knave of Hearts—the first one to appear.

(Enter Knave of Hearts*)*

KNAVE: I'm called the Knave, though not a knave as sometimes understood,
For I am often known as 'Jack,' and Jacks are always good.
I am also jester to the King—yes, *jest* a comic Jack,
For you must know that I'm the only Joker in the pack.

FAIRY QUEEN: And now I'll call Her Majesty—the famous Queen of Hearts,
Whose name is known throughout the land for making lovely tarts.

(Enter Queen*)*

QUEEN: Yes, I'm the Queen, as you can see; I've dignity and grace,
I'm favoured by the Flying Corps when taken by the 'Ace.'
Just why I wed my Mr. King I really cannot think,

204

Although he thinks himself a King, to me he's just a 'kink.'

FAIRY QUEEN: And now His Majesty the King, who ably fills the throne.

(Enter King)

KING: I am the King and no *joking*—whose throne's not overthrown.
Although I've had a peaceful *reign,* I much regret to say
I haven't saved sufficient wealth for my own *rainy* day.
My crown is worth but *half a crown*—enough to make me cuss,
I fear as King I've missed my mark.

QUEEN, KNAVE: And so say all of us.

FAIRY QUEEN: Now let me warn you one and all before I say farewell.
Upon you all a sinful witch has cast an evil spell.
So should you feel that danger's near, pray do not be afraid,
Just summon me and with all speed I'll hasten to your aid.

(Exit Fairy Queen R.)

KING: Now that's what I call a nice, kind girl.

KNAVE: I wonder if she's walking out with anyone for regular?

QUEEN: I think she should wear a few more clothes this change-able weather.

KING: Remember, dear, she is a fairy and you can't expect her to go about in red flannel undies like you wear, and I don't think her union would allow it.

KNAVE: But she said we had only to think and she'd appear. What can I think about?

KING: You mean what can you think *with*.

QUEEN: *(To King)* You should talk. When brains were being given out you must have waited in the wrong queue—they gave you brawn instead of brains.

KING: What an *awful* idea.

205

KNAVE: Not *awful*—you mean *offal*.

KING: Now let us finish with this brains trust talk and get back to the fairy. I've taken quite a fancy to her.

QUEEN: You—you old wreck. You should know better.

KING: But I always had an eye for beauty—that's why I married you, my dear.

QUEEN: Sorry, I can't return the compliment.

KING: But, remember, beauty is but skin deep.

QUEEN: Well, it's quite time you were skinned.

KNAVE: But surely a royal *heir* should not be compared with a *rabbit*.

KING: *(To Queen)* You say I should be skinned. I'm already *skinned out*. I haven't a *bean*. How about you, Knave?

KNAVE: I'm the wrong sort of Jack for beans—you want Jack and the *Bean*stalk.

KING: It is so undignified for a King to be hard up. Only yesterday I went to open a country bazaar and had to borrow a shilling for my fare home.

KNAVE: A *shilling* for a *sovereign*—sort of *quid* pro quo.

QUEEN: You should have raffled yourself in the bran tub and driven home on the proceeds.

KING: But I didn't; I came home on shanks's pony.

KNAVE: You might have saved your feet by wearing stilts to cover the King's *highway*.

KING: This is no time for foolery. I must fill my empty coffers. What new tax can I introduce?

QUEEN: Try a tax on *gold* and *silver*.

KNAVE: Or a *tin tacks*.

KING: They are already on points.

KNAVE: I have it—put a tax on cats.

KING: *(Aside to Knave)* I'm already married to one.

QUEEN: Oh, so that's what you think I am.

KING: No, dear, I...

QUEEN: If I were a cat I should at least have a fur coat of my own, which is more than I can say now.

KING: All in good time, my dear, and you shall have rings on your fingers and bells on your toes. *(To Knave)* I suppose you don't happen to have a little nest egg you'd like to loan your royal master.

KNAVE: I'm sorry, but my nest egg has become addled. It is so dry now. It's almost dehydrated.

QUEEN: Oh, the language!

KNAVE: Remember, I have received no wages for over two years.

KING: Now why bring that up?

KNAVE: Well, addled eggs are hard to *keep down.*

KING: Are you talking of eggs or emetics?

QUEEN: Something must be done or we shall soon be out of house and home, if we don't keep up our payments with the building society.

KING: But we must have a home.

KNAVE: Let's call at the baker's and get a *small cottage.*

KING: A truce to all this idle talk—let's start off at the double,
And ask the royal orchestra to help us *air* our trouble.
(Trio. Air: 'She was a dear little dicky bird')
We are a poor lot of nincompoops,
All without a cent,
Through lack of L.S.D. we cannot pay the rent
We hope ere long to live upon better terms,
Once we belonged to the wealthy birds,
But now we're just three of the worms.

(Optional Dance. Exeunt King, Queen and Knave)

(Enter Princess)

PRINCESS: A sad Princess indeed; I am without a friend to cheer me.
On this my birthday, all alone, with no companion near me.
Though in a palace grand I dwell, I cannot yet discover—
A soul mate who would willingly proclaim himself my lover.
If only in my life I had some little real affection,
Just true love in a cottage would, to me, be just perfection.

(Re-enter King)

KING: Oh, dear! Oh, dear! I'm in a mess—now where's my charming daughter?

(Re-enter Princess)

Ah, there you are—now come and kiss your Daddy as you oughter.

PRINCESS: To-day's my birthday, Daddy dear, you promised me a present.

KING: *My present* funds, I much regret, are anything but pleasant.
I'll make amends some other day—don't think I'm getting crafty—
But, truth to tell, my bank account is very overdrafty.

PRINCESS: You promised me all sorts of things, first one thing, then another.

KING: I've been talking matters over, dear, with your delightful mother. We think it's time that you should wed. We want to get you off, dear.

PRINCESS: But tell me, who am I to wed?

KING: The famous Yellow Dwarf, dear.

PRINCESS: The Yellow Dwarf! Oh, no—no!! NO!!! The thought of that is loathsome.

KING: But think, dear, he has wealth to burn, and p'raps he'll

208

give us *both some.*

PRINCESS: I'll only wed the man I love. I vow I'll have no other.

KING: Now listen to your dad's advice. But, look! here comes
your mother.

(Enter Queen*)*

QUEEN: I hope our daughter's pleased to learn about her
wealthy suitor.

KING: To tell the truth, I'm much afraid our suitor doesn't suit
her.

QUEEN: *(To* Princess*)* Is that true what your father says? I
think you most ungrateful.

PRINCESS: You're asking me to wed that dwarf—to me he's
simply hateful.

QUEEN: He's coming here to tea to-day—I've just received his
letter.
I'll make some tarts in shapes of hearts, there's nothing he
likes better.
(To King*)* Now, Adolphus, come along—don't stand there
like a dummy. I'm wanting you to give a hand.

KING: I'd prefer a hand at rummy.

(Exit Queen. *Followed by* King*)*

PRINCESS: The very thought of wedding him just fills my heart
with sorrow.
Perhaps a song might cheer me up and bring a bright tomorrow.

(Song for Princess. *Almost any love ballad could be introduced here. At finish of song she retires up stage and sits on
seat.)*

Alone I'll rest, perchance to dream, and hope when I awaken
My future may bring happiness and love won't be forsaken.

*(*Princess *closes eyes and sleeps. Soft music)*

(Enter Fairy Queen*)*

FAIRY QUEEN: Take heart, Princess, and never fear—you've
  brighter days ahead.
  What ere may come, I promise you that dwarf you shall not
  wed.
  Upon the tarts the Queen has made I'll place my magic
  spell,
  And he who eats those tarts shall be the one to love you
  well.

(Exit Fairy Queen*)*

*(Knave enters. He is carrying a dish of tarts. He picks one
off the dish and is about to eat it, but conveys it is too hot.
Replaces the dish)*

KNAVE: I stole these tarts, they looked so nice; I couldn't just
  resist them.
  But all the lot are much too hot to get into my system.
  I'll put them by the palace gates and leave them till I *go out,*
  And when the air has blown them cool then *I* will have my
  blow out.

(He catches sight of Princess, *who is now showing signs of
awakening, and makes a hasty exit)*

PRINCESS: I've had a dream that seemed to tell I've happiness
  in store,
  And I shall wed the man I love with joy for evermore.
  And yet I fear I'll never feel that pang of Cupid's dart,
  But still I'll hope and wander on and nurse my aching heart.

(Exit Princess*)*

(Enter Queen *hurriedly. She is followed by* King. *They both
appear very agitated. They rush round stage looking every-
where as they speak their lines)*

QUEEN: The tarts have gone—where can they be? That is
  the vital question.

KING: I only hope that the sneaking thief will die of indigestion.

QUEEN: How dare you say a thing like that! Why no one could

be prouder—
Of making tarts as light as mine and not use baking powder.

KING: I know, my dear, they're always light—I sometimes
have a feeling—
That one day they will float around and cannon off the
ceiling.

QUEEN: What's to be done?—the noble dwarf may be here
any minute.

KING: To coin a Spoonerism, dear, he'll have to 'bear
and grin it.'

QUEEN: Without the tarts to give our guest we can't make
a com*plete start.*

KING: We'll tell him that our dear princess would make
a perfect *sweet-tart.*

QUEEN: Now come, let's have another look. Now do your best.

KING: I *am dear.*

*(In their haste in running about stage they barge into each
other)*

KING: We must be in a one-way street—we've caused
a *traffic jam* dear.

*(They both continue to bustle around stage as they sing the
following lines)*

(Air: 'Oh where, oh where has my little dog gone')

QUEEN: Oh where, oh where have my lov'ly tarts gone,

KING: Oh where, oh where can they be?

QUEEN: They were extra large and I've used all my marge:

BOTH: Oh what shall we give him for tea?

(Exeunt King *and* Queen *hurriedly)*
(Change to exterior)

211

(After the two courtiers have turned centre-piece they both stand with bowed heads as Yellow Dwarf *enters from side of stage)*

YELLOW DWARF: Begone! I wish to be alone

(Exeunt courtiers)

I am here upon a mission: To win the fair princess's hand and fulfil my ambition. And so I go to win my prize, for happiness I'm heading. With all my heart and wordly wealth I'll plan an early wedding.

*(*Dwarf *makes exit R. of centre-piece.* Knave *slowly appears from left side. He still has plate of tarts in his hand. He places this by side of gate)*

KNAVE: I'll leave these tarts awhile to cool and then I'll start to raid 'em:
    I've always said the Queen made tarts as nice as mother made 'em.
    They always told me when at school that I was good at crammin'
    There's nothing I like cramming more than tarts with lots of jam in.
    I think perhaps before I start I'll sing a little ditty,
    And if I don't get your applause I know I've got your pity.

(Song. Air: 'I do like a nice mince pie')

I do like a nice jam tart,
I do like a nice jam tart.
Don't like spice—don't like rice
Don't like tapioca.
But I do like a nice jam tart,
That is my only vice,
Oh! I do like a nice jam tart,
'Cos it's s'nice; s'nice; s'nice.

(Exit Knave*)*

*(*Valentine *enters. He is wearing a long ragged overcoat and carries a tray of china trinkets slung around his neck. Music for his entrance might be a few bars of 'The Wandering Minstrel,' from the 'Mikado')*

VALENTINE: Who'll buy! Who'll buy! my china ware?
My trinkets are beyond compare,
I travel daily with my tray,
Seeking buyers on my way.
Who'll buy! Who'll buy!

*(He goes up to gate and catches sight of tray of tarts left there
by* Knave*)*

Why what is this—I'm much afraid—
I have a rival in my trade.

*(Picks up tray and looks at tarts. He eats a tart. Then replaces
plate, putting other tarts on his tray)*

But no—I see on second look—
The work of some domestic cook.
To me they have a strong appeal,
Such jam tarts make a tasty meal.
Exquisite taste—a sheer delight,
Agreeable to my appetite.
Such toothsome fare I've never known,
'Twill surely keep my voice in tone.
A kindly spot I here discern—
I'll wander on—but soon return.

(Exit Valentine *singing. He might introduce here 'The Pedlars'
Song.'*

*(*Knave *re-enters from behind gate. He picks up plate. Shows
signs of dismay and bursts into tears)*

KNAVE: Some horrid thieves have had my tarts, if only I could
spot 'em,
Now fancy stealing things like that—but still that's how I
got 'em.
I've been promising my tummy it was in for something tasty,
And now I'll have to eat my words—I was a bit too hasty.
But never mind, I'll go without, although it's been unnerv-
ing,
I only hope those tarts have gone to someone more deserv-
ing.
I'll never steal a thing again, not even if I'm dying,

213

(Holds out extended finger, then passes it across his throat)

See that's wet. See that's dry. I'll cut it if I'm lying.

(Exit Knave*)*

INTERIOR

(Enter King *and* Queen. *They back on to stage bowing in the* Yellow Dwarf*)*

KING: All welcome to our honoured guest. We give a hearty greeting.

QUEEN: This is indeed a royal treat for this auspicious meeting.

YELLOW DWARF: Your kind words I appreciate: I do so most sincerely; I have come here on a happy quest.

KING: We understand that clearly.

YELLOW DWARF: I seek to win your daughter's hand and gain her life's affection,
A prouder man I then should be—if you have no objection.

QUEEN: We'd gladly call you son-in-law, of that I do assure you.

KING: There's no one in the royal court that we would put before you.

QUEEN: Now pray be seated while I go and fetch our charming daughter.

(Exit Queen*)*

*(*Dwarf *sits on throne chair. He appears to be quite unconcerned as the* King, *hot and bothered, speaks the following.*

KING: Er—the weather's turned out nice again—the wind's in the right quarter.
I suppose you never—er—but no—on second thought you wouldn't.
I often wonder if you like to—but there, of course, you couldn't.
The ladies seem a long time gone, no doubt they're titivating,
But there, they always seem to like to keep us fellows waiting.

Ah, here they come all bright and gay, just smiling at each other.
My girl's a prize and every day she grows more like her mother.

(Queen and Princess *enter. The* Princess *appears very reluctant, and is almost being pulled in by the* Queen.*)*

QUEEN: Now then, Clarice, come along, give welcome to our guest dear.

KING: Remember all that I have said, so try to look your best, dear.

(Princess walks towards C. Dwarf *rises and bows.)*

QUEEN: *(To* King*)* We'd better let them be alone to do their bill and cooing.

KING: I only hope she'll woo and coo and save her dad from ruin.

(Exeunt King *and* Queen*)*
(Dwarf advances to Princess. Princess *shrinks back)*

YELLOW DWARF: Sweet vision of my heart's delight,
Come listen to my plea,
I ask you to share my life,
I beg on bended knee.
I offer you my worldly wealth,
If you but say the word,
Come give your answer now, sweet maid.

PRINCESS: The whole idea's absurd. I'd rather be a beggar's wife—if love was in my heart.

YELLOW DWARF: *(In slight anger)* So I am refused.

PRINCESS: You are indeed.

YELLOW DWARF: And so I will depart.
I think you'll live to rue this day.

PRINCESS: That, time alone will tell,

My final answer you have had—
There's nothing more—farewell.

(Exit Dwarf. Princess *makes exit in opposite direction)*

EXTERIOR

*(*Witch *enters just as* Dwarf *emerges from behind gate)*

YELLOW DWARF: So once again, you wretched witch, you've
  failed in your endeavour—
  To place me on the royal throne, so leave me now for ever.
  The Princess has refused my hand—my hopes have all been
  blighted,
  Though you vowed that your evil powers could get my
  wishes righted.

WITCH: I did my best. If you but knew, my powers would surprise you. Give me just one more chance.

YELLOW DWARF: No. Henceforth I despise you.

WITCH: I warrant if you turn on *me* then *you* shall be the
  cursed one.

YELLOW DWARF: Of all the witches I have known you've
  proved to be the worst one. I hope we never meet
  again—you wretched necromancer. Away I say.

WITCH: Just one more chance!

YELLOW DWARF: No, no—you've had my answer.

(Exit Dwarf*)*

WITCH: And so my powers have failed at last. It's time that I
  repented.
  I'll end my days like other folk, and may I die contented.

(Exit Witch*)*

(The distant voice of Valentine *singing his Pedlar's song, is
heard. He continues singing during the change of centrepiece)*

INTERIOR

*(*Princess *enters. She stops and turns toward the direction of*
Valentine's *voice)*

PRINCESS: What is that distant voice I hear?—To me it does impart—
A thrill of joy within my soul—a pang within my heart.
It seems to be of one sincere—a man that one could trust,
If I but dare to call to him—but there I feel I must.
I'll beckon from my window here *(Looks off side of stage)* and call him from below.
I feel I am a Juliet and he my Romeo.
(Calling) Hi! Pedlar man! *(*Valentine *stops singing)* Will you come in?
I have a word to say—
About those pretty trinkets you are showing on your tray.

(She turns from window.)

What have I done? I've dared to call a pedlar from the street
Into the royal palace. Have I been indiscreet?

(She turns to side to greet Valentine. *He enters and bows to* Princess*)*

VALENTINE: Oh, why have I been honoured so that you should wish me here?
For you are one of noble birth, while I'm of humble sphere.
A wandering pedlar of the road—just roaming here and there.
Will you, fair maid, accept from me a sample of my ware?

(He hands Princess *a small ornament of Cupid)*

PRINCESS: A little china Cupid, with his bow and arrow, too,
But dare I say this little dart is truly sent by you.

VALENTINE: Well, since I ate a dainty meal that stood by yonder gate—
I've had a strange presentiment that I should meet my fate.

PRINCESS: But, tell me, were they *tarts* you ate—if so, I understand.

VALENTINE: You mean those dainty morsels were the work of your fair hand?

PRINCESS: 'Twas not *my* hand that makes us feel a sort of mutual bond,

217

That spell has been created by a fairy's magic wand.

VALENTINE: You can't think Fate has been so kind to set our hearts aglow?

PRINCESS: I do, indeed.

VALENTINE: Oh, it cannot be. Er . . . perhaps I'd better go.

(He walks toward exit)

PRINCESS: Please do not leave me here alone—I beg of you to stay.
For I have read in story books that love will find a way.

(Duet for Valentine and Princess. Suggestion: *'Love will find a way')*

Duet

(At finish of duet they retire up stage. His arm encircling her waist. King enters and gazes at them in astonishment)

KING: What's this I see? A pedlar man within my royal palace,
I could not think my only child could ever be so callous.
Now then, you two—just break away and give an explanation.
I think that third-class traveller has gone beyond his station.

KING: Oh, daddy, do not be annoyed. I called him from the street, dear,
To come within the palace doors.

KING: I hoped he wiped his feet, dear.
(To Valentine*)* For this intrusion you shall pay. And don't think I am bluffing.
Begone, before I throw you out—you ragged ragamuffin.
(To Princess*)* What will your queenly mother say—the shock, I fear, might kill her,
Though Queen of Hearts her heart is weak. I'll call her now. Priscilla!

VALENTINE: But sire, may I say a word?

KING: You'd better stop your braying.
You wait until my wife arrives, and she'll do all the saying.

(Queen enters. King points to Princess *and* Valentine*)*

QUEEN: Good heavens! What is that I see—our precious daughter spooning.
And with a common pedlar man. *(To King)* Hold me, dear—I'm swooning.

(Queen *falls in* King's *arms. He fans her face)*

KING: This, dear, is more than I can bear—don't give way to prostration,
But take this weight from off my mind and stop their bold flirtation.

(Queen *away from* King)

QUEEN: *(To* Valentine) To you, young man, I'll ask one thing: I want a truthful answer.
If you think you can join our set, I'll tell you now, you can't, sir.

VALENTINE: Your Majesty, I beg of you . . .

KING: No begging is allowed here.

PRINCESS: But, daddy, when you've heard the truth, I'm sure you will be proud, dear.

KING: Oh, fiddlesticks!

QUEEN: And kettledrums! Although I'm no musician.

VALENTINE: I think we may all harmonise when I state my position.

PRINCESS: I do implore you, let him speak, and then you will not doubt him.

QUEEN: All right, young man, then say your piece.

KING: Yes, let's hear all about him.

VALENTINE: In truth, I'm not a pedlar man—I'm blest with wealth and riches.
But money has no charm for me.

KING: *(Rubbing palm of hand)* My palm already itches.
Then tell us why that strange disguise that caused us both to grumble?

VALENTINE: I did it just to see true life among the poor and humble.

(Valentine throws off his ragged overcoat and displays his handsome court dress. All look at him in surprise)

QUEEN: If that's his suit for every day, what must he wear on Sundays?
I've never seen a man before in such delightful undies.

KING: It's time, I think, we called the court—so let the whole lot rally.
Our *court* is rather short just now—in fact, it's like an *alley*.

(Sound of toy trumpet heard off stage. Then Knave enters with trumpet in hand)

KNAVE: Excuse my fanfare being weak—this is my only trumpet.
I got it from a muffin man who's just gone off his crumpet.

PRINCESS: But there is one we have to thank for all this joy of ours,
And that one is our Fairy Queen, possessed of magic powers.

(Fairy Queen enters)

FAIRY QUEEN: 'Twas I who touched those stolen tarts of which our hero tasted.

KING: *(To* Queen*)* So, after all, I'm pleased, my dear, your pastry wasn't wasted.

VALENTINE: I ate one at the palace gates—I could not overlook them.

KNAVE: *(Aside)* Though I still think of what I lost—I'm glad 'twas *he* who took them.

PRINCESS: And I have found true love at last—a joy beyond all measure.

VALENTINE: And I have won a precious jewel—a perfect, priceless treasure.

QUEEN: What of the Yellow Dwarf and Witch? What shall we do about them?

KING: I think we'd better ask them in, we aren't complete without them.

KNAVE: The Dwarf is in the yellow room—the Witch is in the kitchen.
It isn't fair to leave them out. I'll ask the Dwarf and Witch in.

PRINCESS: Our Fairy Queen will wave her wand—for she's so very clever,
And I've no doubt her kindly gifts will make them good for ever.

(Enter Dwarf *and* Witch*)*

*(*Fairy Queen *waves wand as they enter)*

YELLOW DWARF: I promise from my future life I'll shun all vain ambition.

WITCH: And I will cease to curse the world in spite of all tradition.

KING: Well, things have turned out nice again, and all seems bright before us.
So let us all join hand-in-hand and sing our final chorus.

FINALE

(Air: 'Here we are again')

Now we are—*as* we are,
All is right as rain.
If you have all enjoyed our little show—
Put your hands together,
and then go 'yell' for leather,
And sing with us and let your voices go.

(Repeat refrain inviting audience to join in)

»

LITTLE RED RIDING HOOD

(1951)

CHARACTERS:
  Mother Hubbard
  Red Riding Hood
  Fairy Queen
  Witch
  Simple Simon
  Prince
  Granny
  Wolf

Villagers and guests, etc., may be added to
suit conditions.

(Home of Mother Hubbard. Mother Hubbard enters.)

HUBBARD: No doubt you all have heard of me—I'm Mrs.
  Mother Hubbard,
  Who couldn't find her dog a bone when she went to the
  cupboard.
  But now-a-days I'm better off—I'm friendly with my
  grocer—
  Who calls me little Buttercup—our friendship's getting
  closer.
  So now my cupboard's nicely stocked with one thing and
  another,
  I'm sending my Red Riding Hood with presents for my
  mother.
  I quite forgot to tell you that Red Riding Hood's my
  daughter.
  I sometimes call her 'R. R. H.,' it's quicker and it's shorter.
  She's all the world to poor old me—my word she is a sweet
  'un,
  When young I had a pretty face—but now it's got moth-eaten.

223

Ah, you can laugh, but in my youth I was a gay young
  dasher,
I've broken many lovers' hearts—I was indeed a smasher.
But when I wed and settled down I took Mrs. Beeton's book
  in,
And read about the proper way a wife should do her
  cookin'.
The first rock cakes I made for tea turned out a bit too
  rocky,
My husband soon complained of pains and looked a trifle
  crocky.
He gently whispered in my ear—unable to speak louder,
And said 'You must have used cement instead of baking
  powder.'
I asked him to forgive me, but he seemed so undecided,
And late that night he passed away and left me unprovided.
But there, I mustn't get so sad, it's really much too early,
I'd better sing a little song about my little girlie.

*(Any song of the moment can be introduced here, or the fol-
lowing can be used. Air: 'Oh my what can the matter be')*

Oh my where is Red Riding Hood,
She has to go through the shady wood,
With a basket of dainty food—
To take Granny some fish for her tea.
She went off this morning in her Sunday slippers,
To get her dear Granny a nice tin of 'skippers,'
Those sardines I'm sure will have grown into kippers,
If she doesn't soon come back to me.
But there, today's my washing day—I got to put in soak
  a—
Basket full of dirty clothes and dust the tapioca.

(Goes towards Exit R. Voice of Red Riding Hood *heard off L.)*

(Enter Red Riding Hood*)*

RED RIDING HOOD: Mother.

MOTHER HUBBARD: If I'd have known you'd been so long I'd
  have gone myself to fetch 'em.

RED RIDING HOOD: These sardines took some time to get.

224

MOTHER HUBBARD: Did you have to go and catch 'em?

RED RIDING HOOD: No, Mother dear—to tell the truth I lingered
on my way,
And thought about that handsome prince I met the other
day—
When walking through the forest glade 'twas there he
looked at me
I saw the love light in his eyes.

MOTHER HUBBARD: Oh, fiddle-de-de-de,
To think a prince would look at you—a lass of humble
birth,
He'd want to wed a wealthy girl and get his money's worth.

RED RIDING HOOD: They wed poor girls in fairy tales and that
you can't deny,
So even *I* might wed a prince . . .

MOTHER HUBBARD: And little pigs *might* fly.
It's no good building up your hopes and talk of what might
be,

(Goes to side and brings on basket of food)

You must take these things to Granny—she'll be waiting for
her tea.
There's a pot of jam, some bloater paste, a slice of currant
cake,
And a little box of peppermints should she get the tummy
ache.
Now give my love to Granny, and don't forget to say—
I've sent that other half an egg I promised her today.

(Exit Hub. *R.   Soft music)*

RED RIDING HOOD: When I get to that shady wood my joy will
be supreme,
If I perchance should meet again the hero of my dream.

*(She could here introduce a short simple love song. Soft music
to continue as she slowly walks towards Exit L. Fairy Queen to
enter R.—unseen by* Red R. H. F. Q. *follows closely behind as
she says the following lines. The entrance of* Fairy Queen *is
optional)*

225

FAIRY QUEEN: Lead on sweet maid, and do not fear should danger come your way,
The fairies will watch over you for all the live long day.

(Curtains close on Scene 1)

Scene 2. THE FOREST. All that is needed is the trunk of a tree in profile up stage C. This to be large enough to cover opening in curtains and to enable the characters to use it as an entrance. At the opening of the scene, the Witch puts her head round the side of tree and gives a fiendish laugh, then enters.

WITCH: I glory in all sinful deeds—I am a wicked witch,
When I see trouble close at hand my fingers start to twitch.
I curse all lovers old and young—I hate a faithful heart,
I laugh with glee when I succeed in tearing them apart.
I've one companion in these woods—a wolf with hungry eyes,
And with my aid he hopes to get a toothsome little prize.
I hear her name's Red Riding Hood—'tis she I hope to steal—
And hand her to the hungry wolf to have a tasty meal.
'Tis 'bout the time she comes along so I must now away,
And get the wolf in readiness to pounce upon his prey.

(Exit behind tree. Enter Simple Simon L. He carries butterfly net on the end of stick. He swoops it about in the air as though catching imaginary butterflies. Then down stage for his lines)

SIMPLE SIMON: I am simply Simple Simon, but I truly don't think I'm—
The proper sort of fellow for this pretty pantomime.
It's strange why they've included me. But this is my belief—
They've sent me on to give a little comedy relief.
I have to be the funny man, so *should* I make a joke,
I want to hear you laugh so hard as though you're going to choke.
The jokes I have collected I am sure you will agree—
Have fallen from the branches of an ancient chestnut tree.
My first joke is about a man who drank some paraffin,
Then breathed upon a lighted match—since then he's not *benzine*.

(He gives a loud inane laugh after each feeble joke)

This net's for catching butterflies as they all flutter by
And when I have hot toast for tea *I* make the *butter fly.*
    (laughs)
That's not so silly as it sounds—so don't give me the snub,
But butterflies and buttered toast are both a form of *grub.*
    (laughs)
I once thought moths and butterflies were tiny worms with
    wings,
So got myself this little book to read about such things.
It's called 'Hints to young *Moth*-ers,' but find that I've been
    had,
It's all about young babies—I'm too young to be a dad.
    (laughs)
I haven't caught a thing all day, no matter where I've been,
I think some of the butterflies have turned to margarine.
    (laughs)
Now I should like to sing if you will promise me you'll hark,
Don't take me for a nightingale—I'll just sing for a *lark.*
    (Into song. Air: 'Little Brown Jug')

Though Simple Simon is my name,
I can't help that—I'm not to blame,
When I was born the neighbours say—
It was a most unlucky day.
    Ha! ha! ha! He! he! he!
    But I've a sweetheart fond of me,
    She whispers in my ear you see,
    'Little brown *Mug* I do love thee.'
I always think it does me good,
To watch the insects in the wood.
The ants and gnats walk out in pairs,
And talk about their love affairs.
    Ha! ha! ha! He! he! he!
    They're all as happy as can be,
    For once I heard a lady flea—
    Say 'Little brown *Bug* I do love thee.'
I like to be so good and kind,
To all the little things I find,
When I see danger come their way,
I did a good deed yesterday.

Ha! ha! ha! He! he! he!
A buttercup came up to me,
And said 'Please hide me up a tree—
A little brown *Slug* is chasing me.'
I think it's time I got along,
And finished up this silly song,
So to my cottage I will roam,
I'm better off when in a home.
Ha! ha! ha! He! he! he!
It's time you said good-bye to me,
I'm going to have—when I've had tea—
A little tight *hug* on mother's knee.

(The fingers of the Witch's *hand comes round side of tree.*
Simon *looks at them)*

There's somything crawling round that tree I've not collected yet.
I think it is a dragon fly—I'll catch it in my net.

(He cautiously goes towards the fingers as the Witch *puts her
face round side of tree.* Simon *shakes with fear and, shouting*
'Mother,' *rushes off stage.* Witch *enters)*
WITCH: My curses on that silly lad—how dare he interfere—
I cannot trap Red Riding Hood when other folks are near,

(She looks off L.)

And here she comes. Now Mr. Wolf can have a fine repast,
And I have been successful and I've got my wish at last.

(She makes hasty exit behind tree)

*(*Red R. H. *enters L. She drops handkerchief as* Prince *enters
R. She appears nonplussed.* Prince *picks up handkerchief and
hands it back to her)*

PRINCE: O pardon me fair maiden—this I think belongs to you.

RED RIDING HOOD: Oh—er—yes—I must have dropped
it—what a silly thing to do.
In addressing one of Royal blood I can't think what to say,
So, Sire, will you pardon if I journey on my way.

(Red R. H. goes towards exit R. Prince brings her back)

PRINCE: Stay, pretty maid, where goest thou? Say is your journey far?

RED RIDING HOOD: No, Sire, I'm only going to my dear old Grandmama,
Who lives in yonder cottage with the roses round the door,
I daily take her dainty food.

PRINCE: A gracious act I'm sure.
If only there were more such maids with thoughts so good and kind,
A better and much brighter world we very soon would find.

RED RIDING HOOD: I really must be going, Sire, along the winding lane,
And so good-day...

PRINCE: But not *good-bye*. We may soon meet again.

(R.R.H. goes off R. Prince watches her and heaves a sigh, and slowly makes his exit L. Witch comes from behind tree and looks off R.)

WITCH: There goes that cursed little kid—the one I so detest,

(Call off behind tree)

Now hungry wolf here is your chance—this is no time to rest.

(Enter Wolf from behind tree. He should be wearing a tight-fitting costume. Long-fingered gloves to look like claws. Wearing wolf mask. He gives a loud howl as he enters)

WITCH: Look there along the winding lane she slowly wends her way,
You hasten by the narrow path—your victim to waylay.

(Wolf gives angry cry and rushes off R.)

He'll get her yet, and eat her up, then I can laugh with glee,
None can defy a witch's curse...

(Enter Fairy)

229

FAIRY: Have you forgotten me?

WITCH: You silly little fairy elf. To try and thwart my aim.

FAIRY: That's why I'm here,

WITCH: But never fear, I'll spoil your little game.

FAIRY: We fairies have a magic charm . . .

WITCH: But I can cast a spell
My power can defy your charm

FAIRY: That time alone will tell.

*(Exit Witch behind tree. A short dance by Fairy or Fairies can
be introduced here to close scene)*
End of Scene 2

Scene 3. Interior of Grandmother's cottage. Bed up back C.
Granny discovered arranging bed. She unfolds large nightdress, white mob cap, spectacles, etc.)

GRANNY: There's nothing like a comfy bed to keep you from the
cold,
For I often get the shivers now that I am getting old.
I like to keep my nightie neat and cap as white as snow,
In case when I am dreaming I meet somebody I know.
I saw old Mrs. Perkins in my dream the other night,
She was wearing sailor's trousers and she did look such a
fright.
So now I'd better go to bed and wait for Red Riding Hood,
There never was a grand-daughter so kindly and so good.
I long to hear her pretty voice.

(Howl of Wolf heard off stage)

Good gracious, what was that?
It can't be the insurance man. It must have been the cat.

*(Wolf enters slowly. Gran. runs in fear off L. followed by
Wolf. Slam of door heard off. Wolf returns)*

WOLF: I've *locked* the old girl out of sight, in there she's safe
enough,

230

She doesn't suit my appetite, she's much too old and tough.

(Puts on nightcap and nightdress)

So now I'll get into her bed and rest in this disguise,
The features of a hungry wolf no one will recognise *(Gets into bed)*
Now all is set, it must be time Red Riding Hood was here,

(Sound of door latch off stage)

Here comes my prize. I thirst for blood

(Speaking in woman's voice)

come in my little dear.

(Enter Red Riding Hood. She speaks as she enters)

RED RIDING HOOD: Well here I am dear Grandma, with nice things for your tea.
When in the wood I met a Prince, he stopped and spoke to me.

(Turns towards bed)

Ah there you are. Oh Granny dear, you have got great big eyes,

WOLF: The better dear for seeing you my precious little prize.

RED RIDING HOOD: I am sure your ears are bigger than they were the other day,

WOLF: Much better dear for hearing all the things you have to say.

RED RIDING HOOD: But Granny all your teeth have grown, whatever will you do?

WOLF: They'll help me when I start to eat up little girls like you.

(Wolf jumps out of bed. Red R.H. looks on in terror)

At last I have you in my power—you're mine for one and all,

And now I'm going to eat you up

(*Loud cry from* Red R.H. Prince *enters hurriedly*)

PRINCE: Did I hear someone call?

(Wolf *unhands* Red R.H. *She looks at* Prince *in surprise*)

RED RIDING HOOD: Oh, sire, I can't understand how you came
to my aid,

PRINCE: I was guided by a fairy queen I met when in the glade.

(Prince *draws his sword and turns on* Wolf. *He makes several
ineffective thrusts at* Wolf)

PRINCE: Now Mr. Wolf you deal with *me*—it's now *your* turn
to cry,
Take that you fiend, and that, and that—and finally you
die.

(*Makes final thrust at* Wolf *who staggers and falls off by entrance so that stage may remain clear. He turns to* Red R.H.)

The wolf is dead. Now you are safe. I've proved your lucky
star
So now my dear you've naught to fear . . .

RED RIDING HOOD: But where's dear Grandmama?
She must be found (*Calling*) O Granny dear. Are you nowhere about?

(Granny *calling off stage*)

GRANNY: That horrid wolf he locked me *in,* and then he locked
me *out.*

(Red R.H. *runs to side of stage. Sound of unlocking door is
heard.* Granny *enters*)

GRANNY: Oh dear, oh dear, I've had a fright. I thought I'd met
my end,
Some great big 'anamile' came here (*Suddenly stopping and
seeing* Prince) but darling who's your friend?

RED RIDING HOOD: This gallant Prince has saved my life. We
are safe for evermore.

232

PRINCE: *(To* Gran.*)* I fear I had to do the deed beside your cottage door.

GRANNY: Don't worry, sire, about dead wolves who make things look untidy,
I'll get a broom and sweep him up—the dustman calls on Friday.

(Exit Gran.*)*

RED RIDING HOOD: What can I do to thank you for the brave deed you have done?

PRINCE: I only ask that our two hearts may one day beat as one.

(A short love duet could be introduced here)

(Enter Simple Simon *still holding butterfly net)*

SIMPLE SIMON: I've caught the biggest butterfly that you have ever seen,
It's got a lovely pair of wings—I think it is a queen.

(Enter Fairy Queen*)*

PRINCE: It must have been her unseen hand that guided me to you.

RED RIDING HOOD: Oh tell me please, dear fairy queen, can that be really true.

FAIRY QUEEN: Indeed it is for I possess a wondrous magic charm,
'Twas I who sent the Prince to you to keep you from all harm.

RED RIDING HOOD: I thank you for your kindly deed.

PRINCE: And *I* must thank you too,

FAIRY QUEEN: I've only done my duty as good fairies always do.
How glad I was to rescue this young maiden in distress,
A fairy's one ambitions is to bring true happiness.

(Exit F. Queen*)*

RED RIDING HOOD: But what has happened to that witch who cast a wicked spell?

SIMPLE SIMON: The last thing that I heard of her she'd tumbled down a well.
When someone went and fished her out, her face was black as pitch,
She's now beside the old black sow—you can't tell *which* is *witch.*

PRINCE: I have won a precious prize, thanks to the fairies' aid.

*(*Mother H. *enters hurriedly carrying jam pot. She speak to* Red R.H.*)*

MOTHER HUBBARD: My darling you forgot to bring dear Granny's marmalade.

(Suddenly catching sight of others)

What's all this—a party on? Whatever can it mean?

RED RIDING HOOD: It means I'm going to wed the Prince.

MOTHER HUBBARD: Will that make me a queen?

PRINCE: I am going to beg your daughter's hand, and be your future son.

MOTHER HUBBARD: I give consent, although it's sad to lose my little one.

RED RIDING HOOD: Where's Grandma? *(Enter* Gran.*)* Ah, here she is, as busy as can be,

GRANNY: I've been and put the kettle on, you all must stop to tea.

PRINCE: I'll give an invitation—if all of you would care—
To journey to my palace and we'll hold our party there.

(All give signs of joy. Prince *stands by* Red R.H.*)*

MOTHER HUBBARD: *(Aside to* Gran.*)* We are going to the palace.

GRANNY: What, the picture palace?

MOTHER HUBBARD: No.
The palace where the Prince resides, he's asked us all to go.
'Twill make us all feel young again to sing and dance with glee,

GRANNY: If we should play at postman's knock—I hope he chooses me.

MOTHER HUBBARD: *(To* Simple S.*)* You'd better go and wash your face, now look alive *(Pushes* S. Simon*)*.

SIMPLE SIMON: Don't shove.

MOTHER HUBBARD: We'd better go. I think the lovers want to talk on love.

(Exeunt Mother H., Gran., *and* Simple S.*)*

PRINCE: And now you are alone with me. The one whom you belong.
So let us open up our hearts and tell our thoughts in song.

(Love duet from Prince *and* Red R. H. *The following rewritten refrains to 'I think of you, dear' (Western), published Reynolds & Co. would, fit the situation here) Refrain*:

PRINCE: When I see the blossoms swaying gently in the breeze,
I think of you dear, I think of you,
When I hear the turtle doves all cooing in the trees,
I think of you dear, I think of you,
And when I from my daydreams awaken with a start,
Find I've been a victim of a stab from Cupid's dart,
When I think of everything that's dearest to my heart,
I think of you dear, I think of you.

Refrain

RED RIDING HOOD: When I think of the heroes and noble parts they've played,
I think of you dear, I think of you,
When I think of the dangers they meet with undismayed,
I think of you dear, I think of you,
You came to my protection—an answer to my prayer,
And slew that horrid monster when I was in despair,
When I think with whom my future life I'd like to share,
I think of you dear, I think of you.

(They walk slowly toward exit as scene closes)
End of Scene 3

Scene 4. The Prince's Palace. To add a slight idea of grandeur a festoon of gold-paper chains might be hung across the stage. If possible a number of brightly dressed 'guests' might be included to brighten up the scene. This scene should be just a merry romp. The music of 'Here's to the Maiden' might be played during the whole scene, as all dance. At cue, Mother H. enters, she to be wearing some eccentric get-up, such as rose in her hair, brightly coloured shawl, etc. She is followed by Simple S., he might be wearing an ill-fitting dress-suit. Granny follows gaily dressed, wearing paper hat, etc. She slightly raises her skirt and hobbles down stage in an attempt to join in the dance.

GRANNY: *(Shouting)* Whoopee!

MOTHER HUBBARD: Grandma, control yourself. You must have more repose.

GRANNY: I've caught the party spirit, dear, I don't care if it snows.

SIMPLE SIMON: I've got the party spirit, too, and there is no mistake,
I think I took too big a chunk of Prince's tipsy cake.

MOTHER HUBBARD: Fancy using words like 'chunk,' you must be off your chump,
Be more refined and say I only took a lovely lump.
Behave yourself, here comes the Prince with my dear little daughter.
No doubt we'll have to drink a toast.

GRANNY: What, a toast in toast and water?

MOTHER HUBBARD: Be quiet, Gran, please don't forget you're in the palace now,
So when you see the Prince arrive just give a stately bow.

(As Prince *and* Red R. H. *enter they all give a low bow. Gran in doing so falls over. Prince sings to the refrain of 'Here's to the Maiden.' All stand with glasses in hand)*

(Refrain)

PRINCE: Here is a most affectionate toast
    I offer to you as a genial host.

(Into verse as he turns Red R.H.*)*

    Here's to the maiden I met in the wood,
    Here's to the maid of perfection,
    Drink to the health of my Red Riding Hood,
    The maiden who's won my affection.

(Refrain)

ALL: Here's to the lass, sweet little lass
    For beauty and elegance none can surpass.

(Into verse as he turns to Mother H.*)*

PRINCE: Here's to the lady we all have to bless,
    Here's to our dear Mother Hubbard,
    May her stock of eatables never grow less—
    In her most magnificent cupboard.

Refrain)

ALL: Here's to our Mum, merry old Mum,
    Always so cheerful and never looks glum.

(Into verse as he turns to Simple S.*)*

PRINCE: Here's to young Simon though simple they say,
    To him we have to be grateful,
    He saw that old witch was put out of the way,
    Whose curses were getting so hateful.

(Refrain)

ALL: Here's to the lad—simple young lad,
    Although he is simple he isn't too bad.

(Into verse as he turns to Gran.*)*

PRINCE: Here's to Grandmother though humble and poor,
    Has really turned out to be splendid,
    Years she's been keeping the wolf from the door,
    But now that wolf terror has ended.

237

ALL: Here's to old Gran, plucky old Gran,
Who's helped with our story according to plan.

(Into verse as he turns to Fairy)

PRINCE: Here's to the health of our fairy princess,
Who's heart is so kindly and tender,
She came to the aid of a maid in distress,
And summoned a Prince to defend her.

(Refrain)

Here's to our Fay, fair fairy Fay,
May her charms continue for many a day.

(Music stops. Red R.H. comes forward)

RED RIDING HOOD: Now all has ended happily, like all love stories should,

PRINCE: So let all here give one big cheer for dear Red Riding Hood.

(Music starts again as all join in dance for final curtain.)

GOODY TWO SHOES

(1953)

CHARACTERS:
Goody
Tom
Fairy Queen
Squire
Dame Trot
Showman
Nick
Rob

Villagers and school children may be added to suit conditions.

SCENE: 1: Exterior. Goody and Tom enter hand in hand. Goody is carrying a deep basket and small dog A toy dog could be used, but a live one would be more effective.

TOM: I love my sister Goody.

GOODY: And I love you, my brother,
So let us make a solemn vow to always love each other.
We're just two orphans all alone with no one near to guide us,
If only we'd a mother dear to always be beside us.

TOM: Now cheer up, Goody, don't get sad, there's nothing gained by pining,
I once was told that ev'ry cloud has got a silver lining.

GOODY: That may be true but still we two have been a long time waiting
For happiness to come our way—it still seems hesitating.

TOM: But I expect this happiness for which you're fondly yearning—

239

Has gone astray and lost its way or taken the wrong turning.

GOODY: I've been told in fairyland that all the fairies gladly
Will grant a wish to little girls if they are feeling sadly.

TOM: We can't have fairies on the farm; besides they'd not get
use-ter
The shorting of a fat old sow and the crow of our old
rooster.

GOODY: I know the first thing I should wish if I'd a fairy meet-
ing—
Would be a pair of nice new shoes to put my weary feet in.
Do you wonder I'm unhappy with the pair that I am
wearing,
One of them has worn right out and gone beyond repairing.
I hate to wear such shabby shoes with big holes all about
them,
I'll tuck them in my basket here and walk about without
them.

(She takes off her shabby shoes and put them in basket)

TOM: Some day, dear sis, we may be rich and live in wealthy
places,
Then I will buy you such a lovely pair of pretty 'trotter
cases.'
If I could find some millionaires I'd very soon compel
them—
To . . .

GOODY: You must not use long words like that, not knowing
how to spell them,
But look in my big basket here; I've cut out paper letters
To teach each other how to spell, the same way as our bet-
ters.

TOM: Well, start with me.

*(Goody takes paper letters from her basket and places them on
the ground, spelling them out as she does so)*

GOODY: That's T.O.M. It stands for you.

TOM: It looks a rather poor name.
Now spell out G.O.O.D.Y. for that of course is *your* name.

(Goody *places letters G.O.O.D.Y. on ground*)

GOODY: If I could spell out apple pie we might get some for dinner.

TOM: It's many months since we've had one—no wonder I get thinner.

(*Here a number of village children walk across stage all merrily singing 'Come to the Fair,' or any song of this nature*)

GOODY: We cannot join that happy band

TOM: It does seem rather tragic.

Why don't you set your letters out and spell a spell that's magic?
For magic spells I have been told will often bring forth wonders.
Be careful that your spell's correct, so don't make any blunders.

GOODY: All right, Tom. You go and hide, for if I've no one near me,
I'll do my spelling out aloud and hope the fairies hear me.

(*Exit Tom. Goody stands and covers up her eyes with her hands and spells aloud*)

P.L.E.A.S.E.—please I.S.—is T.H.E.R.E.—there A.—a
F.A.I.R.Y.—fairy N.E.A.R.—near.

(*She uncovers her eyes and looks around*)
Perhaps that wasn't loud enough.

(*She is about to cover up her eyes again as* Fairy Queen *enters*)

F.Q.:   But stay! Your fairy's here.

GOODY: Oh thank you, Fairy, ever so for coming to my aid,
I hope I haven't troubled you.

F.Q.:   Don't fear, my little maid,

We fairies like to exercise the power we possess
To give a kindly blessing to all mortals in distress.
What is your wish? For I can grant whatever you may choose.

GOODY: If you don't mind I'd rather like a pair of nice new shoes.

(Fairy *waves wand over* Goody's *basket*)

F.Q.: Your desire shall be granted. Your wish has now come true.
My magic wand has now transformed your old shoes into new.

(Goody *looks in her basket and brings out a pair of bright new shoes, which have been previously hidden there*)

GOODY: Oh isn't that just wonderful! How did they get in there?

F.Q.: That is a fairy's secret that you mortals must not share,
But don't forget those shoes you have possess a mystic charm,
In keeping you in touch with me if you should come to harm—
You've but to rub those magic shoes and send your thoughts to me,
And I will hasten to your aid wherever you may be.

GOODY: Oh thank you! Thank you, Fairy Queen. To me you've been so kind.

F.Q.: So now I have to leave you, but just bear my words in mind.

(*Exit* F.Q. Goody *is gazing at her shoes*. Tom *re-enters*)

GOODY: Brother Tom come to me quick. I've seen a Fairy Queen.
She turned my old shoes into new—the finest ever seen.

TOM: Oh my, you are a lucky girl—you are, and no mistake.
I hope she soon comes back again and brings a fairy cake.

242

GOODY: She said that she would be my friend and keep watch
over me.

TOM: Then I am free to sail away across the mighty sea.
I want to be a sailor lad and lead a life that's grand,
And bring you back a parrot from some distant foreign
land.

GOODY: Well, good-bye Tom, I wish you luck, but while you
are away—
I'll have no one to talk to but my faithful old dog Tray.

TOM: I'll send a picture postcard ev'rytime I go ashore,
And some lovely bits of seaweed just to hang outside the
door.
So off I go. Good-Goody-bye. I shan't be long away.

GOODY: But when might I expect you back?

TOM: About a fortnight from to-day.

(Exit Tom doing the hornpipe as he goes)

GOODY: Although my brother's gone away I do not feel afraid,
For now I know that I can seek the fairy's kindly aid.
No longer have I shabby shoes that caused me such distress.
With my new shoes I feel as proud as any grand princess.

(Soft music to the air of 'Two lovely black eyes')

Two pretty new shoes—such lovely new shoes,
Won't the folks stare when I get to the fair
In my lovely new shoes.

SCENE 2 — AT THE FAIR. *Scene opens with village children dancing round, hand in hand. Or, if possible, a maypole dance could be introduced here. Any country tune,
such as 'The Floral Dance,' should be played. At end of
dance the children to make their exit carrying the maypole,
to leave the stage clear. Enter Showman, in typical get-up
with high hat, etc. He carries a drum which he beats. He
speaks the following lines in a strong raucous voice.*

SHOW: Walk up! Walk up! everyone—all come along and share—
The festive fun and frolic at our famous country fair.
Come show your pluck and try your luck and win a handsome prize,
We've ginger nuts and brandy snaps, a treat for hungry eyes.
Come on the swing and roundabouts and let your voices go,
The more you sing, the more you bring to see a lovely show.
We've everything for everyone, the young 'uns and the old,
Now come along you ladies, come and have your fortunes told.
Try and steer a dodgem car around the motor track,
If you should fall and break your neck you get your money back.
There's a prize for bonny babies, so keep them well awake,
The winner gets a rattle or a little rattle-snake.
We have jellied eels and mussels and shrimps straight from the sea,
You can even smell the briney when you're sitting down to tea.
We have fun and games and whats-er-names and other things besides,
So if you're feeling tired you can try our donkey rides.
We have a special show of dogs, no matter what's the breed,
If they've four legs and a tail, they're the only things they need.
No matter if it's thoroughbred, a mongrel, or a pup.
Let dogs delight to bark and bite. Walk up! Walk up! Walk up!

(Exit Showman*)*

(Enter Nick *and* Rob, *Two* Tramps*)*

NICK: I am the villain of the piece,

ROB: and I'm a villain too.

NICK: My name is *Nick*

ROB: And mine is *Rob;* that tells you what we do.

NICK: We start by stealing little dogs,

244

                              then hop away like frogs.

ROB: In fact to put it plainly we're a pair of dirty dogs.

NICK: Now every time we sees a dog that's been let off its lead,
     We drop a bit of liver down and let him have a feed.

ROB: Then if there's no one looking, or its master's turned his
     back,
     We picks the little blighter up and pops him in our sack.

NICK: Then we brush him up, and oil his hair, and make him
     look all smart,
     Then find a poor old geezer who has got a tender heart.

ROB: We say the dog's an orphan and has got nowhere to live,
     And ask her if she'll buy him and how much she will give.

NICK: We tell her that it breaks our hearts to give our dog
     away,
     But if she gives us half a quid our hearts are soon O.K.

ROB: We then make for 'The Spotted Dog' and wet the other
     eye.
     Then slowly journey on our way and sing our daily cry.

     (Into song. Air: 'Daddy wouldn't buy me a bow-bow')

     Anybody want to buy a bow-wow.
     Any sort or any kind of bow-wow.
     If you say the breed you like,
     We'll find that kind of tyke,

                    (Looking off L.)

     But look here comes a bow-wow now.

*(*Nick *and* Rob *hide as* Goody *enters. She has dog in arms.
     Dog has a card round neck marked '1st Prize')*

GOODY: My darling dog. My little pet. I think you are perfec-
     tion.
     Not only did you win first prize but everyone's affection.
     If you could be but human and I could call you lover,
     Without a doubt my aching heart would very soon recover.

(She places dog on stage)

Now you stay there and don't you move and I will take my
    chances,
And sing about those long day dreams I have of sweet ro-
    mances.

*(Any simple love song of the moment to be introduced here.
On last few bars of song Rob and Nick enter on tip toes. They
pick up dog, then make a hasty exit R. At finish of song Goody
turns and sees the dog has gone. She appears to be most distressed)*

GOODY: Oh dear! my little dog's not here. He can't have
    gone astray.
He has been the only friend I've had to help me on my way.
Without my little faithful friend I've no one's love to share,
Could I but seek the fairy's aid. I wonder if I dare?
She said that she would come to me if I were in distress,
And with her magic power she would bring me happiness.
She told me I must rub my shoes and wish her to appear:

(She bends down and rubs shoes)

I wonder if she'll hear me now.

(Enter Fairy Queen)

F.Q.:   Your Fairy Queen is here.

GOODY: Oh fairy, I'm in great distress. My little dog has
    strayed,
My only true companion has been stolen I'm afraid.
I can't think he has run away and left me all alone,
For he's the only lover that I have to call my own.

F.Q.: Your little friend shall be restored and he may bring to
    you—
A lover of another kind for ever staunch and true.

(Exit Fairy Queen)

GOODY: My little dog has shown more love than I have ever
    seen,
A lover of a different kind, whatever does she mean?

I do not think real love will come to humble little me,
But I must go on hoping and just simply wait and see.

(A short love song might be introduced here, such as 'Keep on Hoping.' At end of song Young Squire *enters with dog in arms.* Goody *is unaware who he is. She speaks to him in a confused and agitated manner, as she takes dog from his arms)*

Thank you, thank you, ever so—my pet is safe and sound,
But would you kindly tell me where my little dog was found?

SQUIRE: I saw the whole thing happen as I was walking near
I saw two ruffians steal your dog, then quickly disappear.
I caught them up and challenged them, and threatened what I'd do
Unless they handed up the dog I saw belonged to you.

GOODY: You've made me feel so happy now my pet has been restored,
I wish that it were possible to give you some reward.

SQUIRE: Pray do not mention such a thing. I thank you all the same.
To me it's been a pleasure.

GOODY: Please tell me, what's your name?

SQUIRE: *(Hesitatingly)* Oh, I'm just a kind of country chap working on the land.

GOODY: But, you speak so like a gentleman, I don't quite understand.

SQUIRE: Perhaps someday I'll tell you more, but now I must depart,
Although I found your precious pet, I fear I've lost my heart.

(Exit Squire)

GOODY: I throught he said he'd lost his heart, and then he looked at me,
If only I could think it true how happy I should be.

(Speaks to dog in her arms)

247

You have no need to get jealous. I have told you once be-
   fore—
For you I have a mothers' love—could anyone want more?
Now I must take great care of you and keep you on the
   lead,
While I go off to Dame Trot's school and teach them how to
   read.
With my basket full of letters I am doing very well,
Not only do I teach them words, but show them how to
   spell.
But I fear a spell's come over me of quite a different kind,
The vision of a handsome youth still lingers in my mind.
Although we must not tarry here—it's time we got along,
I might just spare one moment for a tiny little song.

   (Song. Air:'I'll be your sweetheart')

   I'd be his sweetheart,
   If he would be mine,
   All my life I'd be his Valentine.
   Ever together—no drifting apart
   Hope that I may, some day,
   Call him my own sweetheart.

SCENE 3 — DAME TROT'S SCHOOL ROOM.
*Blackboard on easel R., wooden form up back. Small table
containing books, etc. This scene, as a contrast to previous
scenes, to be of the rough-and-tumble order and taken in
quick action. Scene opens with a number of boys and girls
seated on form all chanting their multiplication tables in a
sing-song voice 'Twice one are two, twice two are four,' etc.
Timmy Tickle, the bad boy of the school, is standing by
blackboard, on which is a badly-drawn face. He is writing
in large chalk letters T.I.T.C.H.E.R. All the other children
laugh and point to* Timmy.

ALL: *(Calling)* Silly kid, he can't spell teacher.

TIM: Who can't?

ALL: You can't.

248

TIM: All right, I know *(Re-writes on board T.A.T.S. Children laugh)*.

(Dame Trot heard off stage)

ALL: Here comes teacher.

(Enter Dame Trot with cane in hand)

ALL: *(In sing-song voice)* Good morning, dear teacher, good morning to you.

TROT: *(Looking at blackboard)* Who did that?

ALL: Timmy Tickle.

TROT: Come out. Hold out your hand.

(Tim hesitates. Trot takes hold of his hand and holds it out. She brings down cane and hits her own hand. She hops round stage holding her hand as though hurt. All the children hide their laughter.)

As I have always said, it pains me to give you the cane.

TIM: Serve you right.

TROT: Who said that?

ALL: Timmy Tickle.

TROT: Come out, Tim. Hold out your hand.

(Tim has a large clean wooden spoon up his sleeve. He holds handle portion of spoon up sleeve letting spoon portion be seen extended from same. This should look like his hand. Trot gives spoon a smack with cane. Tim shouts as though hurt. Pulls spoon out of sleeve and laughs behind Trot's back)

Now what shall we take this morning?

ALL: A half holiday.

TROT: Nothing of the sort. We will start with a test on general knowledge. Now who was it signed the Magna Carta? Come, come. Who signed Magna Carta?

PUPIL: Please teacher it wasn't me.

TROT: Of course not. It was King John. Now who was it?

TIM: King Kong.

TROT: Now where is the *Miss*issippi?

TIM: With her husband, *Mister* Sippi.

TROT: You're wrong. Who was Noah's wife?

TIM: Joan of *Arc*.

TROT: You ignoramus! Who came after Charles the First?

PUPIL: Charles the Second.

TROT: Clever girl. Now who came after Charles the Second?

TIM: Charlie's Aunt.

TROT: Wrong.

TIM: Charlie Chaplin.

TROT: Nothing of the such-which. What did King Bruce say to the spider?

TIM: Get up them stairs.

TROT: No. He said try, try, try again. Now we'll try mental arithmetic. Ten and four?

PUPIL: Fourteen.

TROT: Right. Two and six?

TIM: Half-a-crown.

TROT: Who said that?

ALL: Timmy Tickle.

TROT: Come out. *(Tim comes out and turns his back to Trot to receive the cane. Trot hits him with cane. Tim brings slate from under his coat at back, grins and sits down.)* Now, children, what is a piece of land surrounded by water called?

ALL: An island.

250

TROT: Correct. Now what is the name of a piece of water surrounded by land?

TIM: A puddle.

TROT: Wrong. Something bigger than a puddle.

TIM: A football pool.

TROT: No. The answer is a lake. Now who was William of
Orange?

TIM: The answer is a lemon.

TROT: Silly boy. Can you spell lemon?

TIM: L.U.M...

TROT: Who can spell lemon?

PUPIL: L.E.M.O.N.

TIM: *(Aside)* Suck it and see.

TROT: Who can spell pomegranate?

PUPIL: P.O.M.E.G.R.anit.

TROT: All your spelling is very bad. We must wait until my new
pupil teacher, Goody, arrives with her letters. She will
teach you how to spell. Ah, here she is.

(Enter Goody *carrying her basket of letters)*

Good morning, dear. I think before you start your spelling
class we had better prepare for a visit from the new
young Squire. He has promised to come to-day to give
out the prizes. I want you all to be on your best beha-
viour. Ah, I think I hear him now. *(Goes to entrance)*
Good morning, sir; this way please.

(Enter young Squire. Goody *catches sight of him and appears
to be taken aback)*

SQUIRE: Good morning, children.

ALL: Good morning, Squire.

TIM: *(Aside)* Good morning, squirt.

TROT: Here are the prizes you have so kindly offered to present.

(She hands him books one by one as she reads out the names of those who have to receive them.)

This one is for Gladys Jenkins*(Pupil goes to Squire to receive book)*.

SQUIRE: *(Hands her book)* You are first in history. Clever girl.

TROT: *(Hands him book)* This is for Willie Winkle, for arithmetic. *(Boy pupil arises as before.)*

(Squire turns to Goody)

SQUIRE: So again I meet this little maid of perfect form and feature.
What brings you here?

GOODY: Oh, I am just a humble pupil teacher.

TROT: To me she's worth her weight in gold. No one could find a better.

SQUIRE: I must admit I thought the same the first time that I met her.

(He crosses to Goody and takes her hand)

TROT: *(To children)* Now all of you can go and play, but don't make too much clatter,
I think the young Squire wants to speak on quite a private matter.

(All children run off, taking the form with them, followed by Trot, who takes blackboard to leave clear stage)

SQUIRE: My thoughts are still for you alone. I trust you will believe me,
Though we were strangers when we met.

GOODY: But ·vhy did you deceive me?
You said to work upon the land was what you were prepared for.

SQUIRE: I just said that to make quite sure for me alone you
cared for.

For after all it matters not if one be high or lowly,

It is the feeling of the heart that makes all true love holy.

*(A short love duet to be introduced here. A suggestion: The
refrain of 'If you were the only girl in the world.' At finish of
duet they saunter off L. Trot hurries on R. She is followed by
children, all shouting as they enter)*

TROT: Oh dear! Oh dear; What's all this noise? Who's causing
this commotion?

ALL: It's Goody's brother, Sailor Tom, from off the mighty
ocean.

(Enter Tom dressed as sailor)

TOM: Now gather round, you boys and girls and listen to my
story,

As how I swept the mighty main and revelled in my glory.

Since last I left my native land I've been the whole world
over,

I'll tell of my tramp-steamer trip since I pushed off from
Dover.

We sailed at first to Timbuktu—then on to the Bahamas,

And saw the people living there all wearing silk pyjamas.

We next put in at Zululand, but couldn't find a Zulu,

So went ashore at Singapore, then on to Honolulu.

A storm arose, our plates got smashed, so off we went to
China,

And got some jugs and Toby mugs, then sailed for Caro-
lina.

The captain thought he'd change his course and tooks us to
Alaska,

He caught a chill, the mate got ill, so we made for Madagas-
car.

That afternoon the captain cried: 'We are due at Gibral-
tar,'

But our steering gear came over queer and landed us at
Malta.

Said the bosun's mate: 'Let's try New York, and get there with
out stopping.'

253

So on we sped, full steam ahead, but found ourselves at
Wapping.
And that's my story of the sea—you know I'd not deceive
you,
And now you know just where I've been

CHILDREN: But none of us believe you.

TOM: You disbelieving lot of brats. What makes you have such
bias—
Against the name of Truthful Tom

PUPIL: It should be Ananias.

(Enter Goody *with* Squire*)*

TOM: Ah, here's one who believes in me. My own devoted sister.

GOODY: Hullo, Tom. A welcome home

TOM: But, Goody, who's your Mister?

SQUIRE: Will you allow me to explain? We'll soon know one
another,
In time to come I hope that you will know me as a brother.

(Enter Dame Trot*)*

TROT: You seem to be progressing well, providing no one stops
you.

TOM: But, Goody, who'll look after me?

GOODY: P'raps Dame Trot will adopt you.

TROT: Come to my arms, my bonny boy, come kiss your Aunty
Trotty.

TOM: In front of all these kiddies here, they'll think we both are
dotty.

GOODY: And now our story's ended and we've reached the final scene.
For all my happiness I have to thank our Fairy Queen.
I'll send my wish to bring her here and join this merry
throng.

254

(Bends down and rubs shoes. Fairy *enters)*

FAIRY: I'm here in answer to your call I hope there's nothing wrong.

GOODY: No. Everything has ended well, and all are satisfied.

SQUIRE: It was through your kindly action I have found my future bride.

GOODY: Please summon all the others here and beg them to remain,
And join our happy party in our musical refrain.

(Fairy waves wand as all other characters enter, including Goody's dog)

FINALE

(Air: 'The man who broke the bank at Monte Carlo')

Now we've reached the time in pantomime—
To make our final call,
And to thank you one and all,
The big ones and the small,
Before we go we'd like to know—
If you've all enjoyed our little show,
If so just clap your hands for Goody Two
Shoes.